Questions of Truth

Questions of Truth

Fifty-one Responses to Questions about God, Science, and Belief

John Polkinghorne
Nicholas Beale

Book design by Drew Stevens
Cover design by designpointinc.com

First edition
Published by Westminster John Knox Press
Louisville, Kentucky

This book is printed on acid-free paper that meets the American National Standards Institute Z39.48 standard. ♾

PRINTED IN THE UNITED STATES OF AMERICA

09 10 11 12 13 14 15 16 17 18 — 10 9 8 7 6 5 4 3 2 1

Library of Congress Cataloging-in-Publication Data

Polkinghorne, J. C.
Questions of truth : fifty-one responses to questions about God, science, and belief / John Polkinghorne & Nicholas Beale. — 1st ed.
p. cm.
Includes bibliographical references and index.
ISBN 978-0-664-23351-8 (alk. paper)
1. Theology, Doctrinal—Popular works—Miscellanea. I. Beale, Nicholas. II. Title.
BT77.P65 2009
230—dc22 2008022164

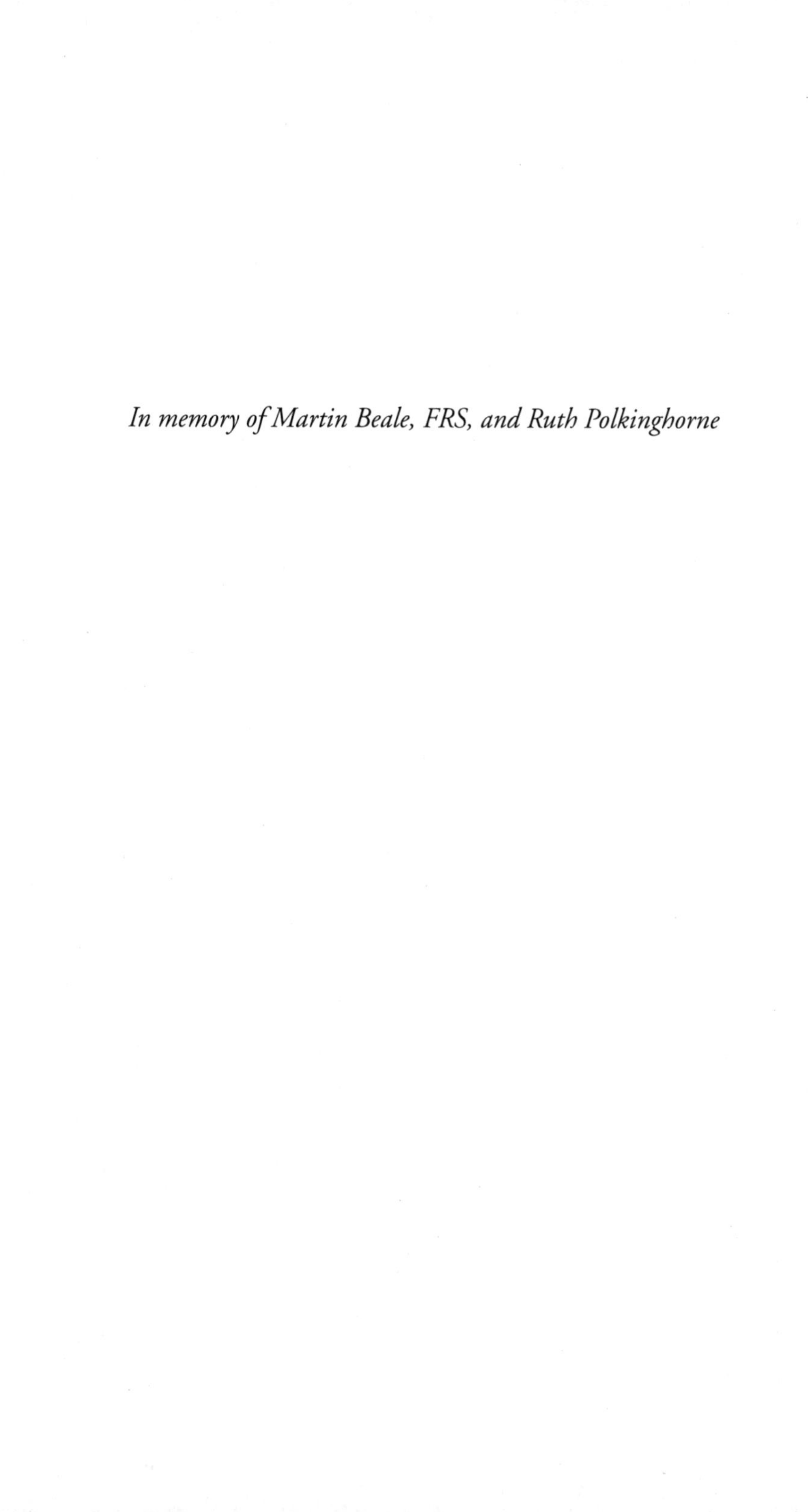

In memory of Martin Beale, FRS, and Ruth Polkinghorne

Contents

Foreword

Cambridge academic eyebrows were raised in 1979 when the distinguished quantum physicist Professor John Polkinghorne resigned from his chair in order to start training as an Anglican priest. Since then he has become well known for a series of books on science and religion. Although not personally online, his ideas have generated worldwide interest and discussion on the Internet through a Web site set up and managed by Nicholas Beale, his onetime mathematical student at Trinity College and long-standing friend and colleague. Nicholas Beale has an outstanding reputation as a management consultant with particular expertise in information technology and was elected Freeman of the City of London in 1996. He is well known for his staunch support of Christianity.

Between them, John and Nicholas have responded to the many questions and issues raised on the Web site, and their different backgrounds and perspectives combine to generate a powerful dialogue covering most aspects of contemporary faith that are of serious concern to those who seek answers to the eternal questions of what it means to be human and the purpose of our existence.

Our culture these days seems to have little room for the sacred. It is widely thought that religion is out of date and irrelevant and has no place in our scientific age; that faith is superstitious nonsense that should have been left behind in kindergarten. John Polkinghorne, on the other hand, argues that science and religion are not in conflict—they are, in fact, complementary, and both are vital for the deepest understanding of our place in the universe. I share this view, along with many other scientists, and believe that physics, perhaps the most materialistic of the pure sciences, actually conditions our thinking in such a way as to help us to be more, rather than less, receptive towards religious mysteries. If rational common sense can be a bad guide to scientific truth, how much more so might it be towards religion? For example, the simplest piece of matter, a hydrogen atom, cannot be accurately described without including the effects caused by the cloud of virtual particles with which it is surrounded. There is no such thing as truly empty space. Quantum theory predicts that even a perfect vacuum is filled with a multitude of particles that flash into and out of existence much too rapidly to be caught by any detector. Yet their existence modifies the motion of electrons orbiting protons in a calculable way that has been verified by direct observation. The ghostly presence of virtual particles defies rational common sense and is nonintuitive for those unacquainted with physics. Religious belief in God, and Christian belief that God became Man around two thousand years ago, may seem strange to common-sense thinking. But when the most elementary physical things behave in this way, we should be prepared to accept that the deepest aspects of our existence go beyond our common-sense intuitions.

Tony Hewish

Preface

I have chosen to be electronically disconnected from the world, but for many years Nicholas Beale has kindly run a Web site concerned with my writings and ideas. An important feature of the site is that it incorporates an interactive facility by means of which users can raise issues and pose questions. Nicholas not only drafts replies, but quite often he refers the matter to me, and I can then add my own comments. Over the years we have built up an archive of the issues that are of concern to people and the responses that we have made to them. This book draws heavily on the insights that we have gained in this way. We hope that its question-and-answer format will be of interest to many and enable them to benefit from a conversation that has certainly been of value to us. Sometimes we offer a single response, and sometimes we each have our own say. Though we are in basic agreement about many things, there are also differences of style and perspective between us. After all, binocular vision is better than monocularity. Three long appendixes give technically careful discussions of three topics of central importance to our argument. They have been compiled by Nicholas in consultation with appropriate experts, and I would like to express my appreciation of the valuable work he has done to achieve this.

At the end of each chapter we provide suggestions for further reading. These are by no means meant to be exhaustive, but they represent a reasonable selection of works that we believe will be found helpful.

I have known Nicholas since he was an undergraduate at Trinity College, Cambridge, where I was then a young don, and I would like to thank him for his generosity in initiating the Web site and keeping it going so effectively.

We write as Christians and necessarily from that faith perspective. We are aware that other faith traditions also are concerned with the issues that we discuss. While we wish to listen to what they have to say, it would not be appropriate for us here to attempt to speak for them. We both wish to thank Dr. Wang-Yen Lee for his invaluable help in the organization and editing of this material. His efficiency and commitment have been essential to the project's completion. We are also very grateful to colleagues who have read and commented on drafts of sections of the book: specifically Prof. Martin Rees, PRS, and Rev. Dr. Rodney Holder on appendix A, Rev. Dr. Fraser Watts and Prof. Peter Clarke on appendix B, and Prof. Simon Conway Morris, FRS, and Prof. Martin Nowak on appendix C. We are enormously grateful to Professor Tony Hewish, FRS, for his foreword. Nicholas and I take full responsibility for any errors that remain.

John Polkinghorne

Introduction

What does it mean to say that the sky is blue? Is it true? Why?

At one level, it is a question about physics, and there is a fascinating story to be told that can be explored down to the level of quantum mechanics. But many other levels of understanding are relevant even to this apparently simple question. For example, there are philosophical issues about what "the sky is blue" means: The sky is not blue all the time. Sometimes it looks black, red, white, or grey. How do I know that what I mean by "blue" is the same as what you mean by "blue," and so forth? Cultural and poetic associations also give whole new layers of meaning: Suppose I say that the (blue) sky is the same color as my mood, or my blood. These statements are obviously false if taken literally.

The sky is not blue on every planet. Our blue sky depends on properties of our atmosphere, which in turn depend on some of the remarkable characteristics of Earth. Both Jupiter and the moon help shield us from frequent large-scale impacts. The composition of our atmosphere has been largely shaped by biological activity. The earth's magnetic field shields us from high levels of cosmic radiation. The color of the sky also depends on the distance we are from the sun. Planets on which any intelligent life-form resembling humans would be likely to evolve would probably have a blue sky, so in an important sense the sky is blue because we are here to observe it. Hence for a Christian, a fuller account of why the sky is blue would connect with what we see as the loving purposes of God.

No one has asked us why the sky is blue, but over the years people from all over the world have e-mailed us questions relating to science and religion. To the ones that raised particularly significant issues, Nicholas has given a preliminary response and then faxed the question and his response to John, who has added his comments. The results have then been e-mailed to the questioner and posted on the Web. For this book we have taken fifty-one questions, based on those that we have been asked, and have provided revised and expanded responses. We hope that readers will follow their own paths through the book, dipping into the questions that interest them and looking at the additional material we provide where they are moved to do so. We've tried to give definitions of any technical terms that we use in the glossary at the end. We're offering responses rather than giving answers, and we'd be surprised if anyone fully agreed with everything we have written. But even after decades of reflection on these topics, we've found the process of bringing these responses together instructive, and we suspect that however well-informed a reader is, there will be some new and interesting material.

Once we have understood the meaning or meanings of a statement, sometimes it is possible to show its logical falsity. For example, the statement that "all true statements can be scientifically proven" *cannot be true*, both for the rather obvious reason that the statement cannot be scientifically proven, and for a deeper, though related, reason due to Gödel's analysis of the subtleties of self-referring statements. Similarly, if God is the ultimate Creator, it is logically impossible that God could in turn be created. To ask, "Who created God?" simply shows that the questioner hasn't fully understood the meaning of the term *God*, which includes the concept theologians call *aseity*—

"Being in itself," with no dependence on anything else for existence. But in most cases, questions of truth, whether about science, religion, or any other field, are more elusive. There are seldom absolute knock-down arguments, one way or another. It is easy to "prove" that nothing can be both a wave and a particle, or that Jesus couldn't have risen from the dead. Yet deep reflection on physics shows that all sufficiently small objects can manifest both wave and particle properties, and even superficial reflection shows that *if* Jesus is the Son of God in anything like the sense that Christians claim, then the resurrection is not only possible but in a certain sense necessary. Conversely, if physicalism is true, then it is pretty clear that the resurrection cannot have happened in the sense claimed by Christians. The judgments about the historicity of the resurrection are inevitably caught up in whether people think that the prior probability of the existence of God is significant. If it is negligible, then the resurrection cannot have happened. If God exists, as we believe, the evidence is pretty strong. In the words of the historian E. P. Sanders, in his book *Jesus and Judaism*, "That the disciples had resurrection experiences I consider historically certain—what they were I cannot say."

If anyone wants to know why we believe that small objects can be both waves and particles; that Jesus did indeed rise from the dead; that the theory of evolution (properly understood as science, not as dogma) is true; that God exists and loves us; that most of the matter in the universe is not composed of protons, neutrons, and electrons; that other people have minds; or why, even without treatment, HIV can take many years to develop into AIDS, then we have to answer, "Come and see." There is a journey of inquiry to be made. It will necessarily involve a set of assumptions and theoretical interpretations, but careful evaluation can lead to the conclusion that there is sufficient motivation to make it rational to commit oneself to the belief in question, both in science and in religion. It is always possible for the skeptic to reject each step with a "but," and many of the skeptic's questions cannot receive absolutely certain answers. "But what is dark matter made of?"—"We don't know." Roger

Penrose's magisterial *The Road to Reality* expounds, in over a thousand pages, the known basic laws of physics from first principles. A determined skeptic could raise objections on almost every page. Or you could read a book like John's *Quantum Physics, a Very Short Introduction,* but there you would have to take a lot on trust.

Similarly, Denis Alexander's *Creation or Evolution—Do We Have to Choose?* sets out in impressive detail both the scientific reasons why we believe in evolution and the sound principles of biblical interpretation, going back at least to the fifth century, that dissolve the superficially apparent contradictions that are mistakenly trotted out. But a determined skeptic could question both the science and theology. Martin Nowak's *Evolutionary Dynamics: Exploring the Equations of Life* explains the HIV/AIDS question, as well as many others, and introduces the necessary mathematics and science. But each step in every argument can be questioned: the issue is whether, taken together, the argument is compelling, worthy of commitment and assent.

We don't attempt to develop everything from first principles. But we hope that this book will be a useful resource to readers from many different backgrounds and positions, and that if people want to explore topics further they will find the references and appendix material useful. Knowledge is in many ways more like a tree than a building, with roots that grow as the branches do. We hope that this tree in the forest of knowledge will provide some interesting paths to climb, and that from its branches readers will be able to glimpse some of the amazing diversity of love and wisdom that underpins the universe as a whole.

1
Leading Questions

This chapter takes nine fundamental issues that underlie the subsequent discourse of the book and, by crystallizing them into nine probing questions, seeks to set the intellectual scene for the many, more-detailed discussions that will follow.

1. Science and Religion

How can there be any meaningful interplay between science and religion? It is said that the universe was written in the language of mathematics, yet the Bible is a mere collection of words.

Mathematics and words are both means for expressing concepts. One uses whatever is appropriate to what one wants to express. Darwin wrote *The Origin of Species* in words and without mathematics because that was the way to get his profound evolutionary idea across. There is nothing "mere" about words—think of Shakespeare and Tolstoy.

Science and religion are certainly concerned with different aspects of reality, so they express themselves differently. Science looks at the world impersonally, treating it as an "it," you might say. This gives it the great secret weapon of experiment, the ability repeatedly to manipulate things to see what happens. In principle, and quite often in practice, if you do not believe what you are told happens, you can check it out for yourself. Consequently, science is often able to express its results in the impersonal language of mathematics. Once we look at reality from a personal perspective, however, the approach has to change. Strict repetition is no longer possible—we never hear a Beethoven quartet exactly the same way twice, even if we play the same disc again. Relationships can no longer be manipulative. If I am always setting traps to see if you are my friend, I shall soon destroy the possibility of friendship between us. That relationship has to be experienced through trusting, not testing. If this is true between human persons, it is scarcely surprising that it is also true of the relationship with the transpersonal reality God. It's no use saying, "If there is a God, let him write me a message on the clouds." God does not play that sort of silly game.

There are, therefore, important differences between science and religion, but there is also an important cousinly relationship. Both are concerned with the search for truth, and both seek truth through a quest for motivated belief. This fact is often obscured by common misconceptions about religious belief. People sometimes say that science is concerned with facts but religion is simply concerned with opinions. That is a double mistake: a mistake about science and a mistake about religion. There are no interesting scientific "facts" that are not already interpreted facts. We might all agree that the pointer on an instrument had turned to 1.7 on the scale, but without using theoretical opinion to say what the instrument is capable of measuring, that would not mean anything significant. Experiment and theory, fact and opinion, intertwine in subtle ways in science. The mistake made about religion is to suppose that religious faith means shutting your eyes and gritting your teeth in a foolish attempt to believe impossible things because some unquestionable authority has told you to do so. Religious belief certainly does not involve committing intellectual suicide. The question of truth is as important to it as it is to science. There are motivations for religious beliefs, but the difference between science and religion means that the kinds of motivation will be different in appropriate ways in the two cases.

For the Christian, this is where the Bible comes in. It is not some divinely dictated textbook giving all the answers, which just have to be accepted without question. It is much more like a laboratory notebook, recording the unique events of divine self-disclosure made in the course of the history of Israel and in the life of Jesus and its astonishing aftermath. The Bible is not a book but a library, with various types of writing in it. There is much history, but there are also symbolic stories that convey truths so deep that only a story form could express them. (That is the true meaning of that much-abused and misunderstood word *myth*, very different from that of a simple fairy story.) In interpreting the Bible it is important to work out what kind of writing one is reading. For example, Genesis 1 is not a literal account of a hectic six days of divine activity, given to save us the trouble of using science to discover the remarkable history of the universe. Instead, it is a piece of theological writing that uses a symbolic story to convey the theological truth that nothing exists except through the creative will of God ("and God said, let there be . . ."). Religion is a multifaceted human activity. It certainly shares with science the intellectual quest for truthful understanding, but it has existential dimensions that have no scientific counterparts—for example, those arising from experience of worship and from commitment to compassionate action. The proper intellectual partner in the conversation with science is not religion as such, but *theology*, whose concern is with intellectual reflection on human encounters with the sacred and with exploration of the nature of God.

One could summarize the difference between science and religion by saying that they are asking different questions about the nature of reality. Science is concerned with the question, How?—By what process do things happen? Theology is concerned with the question, Why?—Is there a meaning and purpose behind what is happening? We are perfectly familiar with the fact that we can ask and answer both questions about the same event. The kettle is boiling because burning gas heats the water. The kettle is burning because I want to make a cup of tea, and will you have one too? We do not have to choose between these two answers, and, in fact, if we are fully to understand the event of the boiling kettle, we need them both. In an exactly similar way we need the insights of both science and religion if we are fully to understand the rich reality we inhabit.

We have every reason to expect that science is able to answer its own questions without having to call on religion, and similarly science cannot answer religion's questions for it. How and why—mechanism and meaning—are distinct inquiries. Nevertheless this does not mean that the answers are completely disconnected. There must be a relation of consonance between them. If I were to say that I want to make a cup of tea and I have just put the kettle in the refrigerator, you would rightly be suspicious. There is therefore the possibility and need for a fruitful dialogue between science and religion as they compare their insights into reality. The rest of this book explores that interaction.

If science and theology are both concerned with the search for truth, they are friends and not foes. Why then is there a common misperception of warfare between "science and religion"? It arises partly from mistakes made in the past. When Darwin published *The Origin of Species* in 1859, many people, both religious and nonreligious alike, opposed him because they thought that acknowledging human kinship with the animals would be fatal to human dignity and destructive of human morality. In our subsequent discussions of evolution we shall seek to show that this was a wrong response. As a matter of historical fact, the mistaken character of this thinking was realized by many religious people at the time. The English clergyman Charles Kingsley and the American botanist Asa Gray were prominent among those who welcomed Darwin's insights from the start. Moreover, the illegitimate importation of nonscientific ideological influences into scientific evaluation has not been the preserve of believers alone. Fred Hoyle embraced the now-discredited steady state theory of cosmology precisely because he feared that what he contemptuously termed the "big bang" theory would support the idea of the universe as a creation.

2. Human Nature

If we admit that our thoughts are dependent on the neural substrate, then how can we possibly say that they determine what we ultimately do?

Human beings are certainly embodied, and there is surely a connection between brain and mind. The effect of a smart tap on the head with a hammer will quickly make the point. However, there are different ways in which the relation between the physical and the mental might be understood.

One is a dualist picture, such as that proposed by Plato and Descartes. It supposes that there are two different parts of a person, the fleshly body and the spiritual soul, made of two different substances, matter and mind. The unresolved problem then is to understand how these two quite separate components manage to interact with each other. In the past, religious thinkers have quite often taken the dualist view, but it is by no means a necessity for religious thought. In fact, it is not very popular in theology today.

Most contemporary theologians believe human beings to be psychosomatic unities, a kind of package deal of matter/mind in a complementary relationship. This would not at all have surprised the biblical writers, who adopted a similar stance, seeing human beings, in a famous and much-quoted phrase, as "animated bodies rather than incarnated souls."

We also take this view, and it by no means implies for us that humans are simply complex automata. Twentieth-century science saw the death of a merely mechanical view of matter. The discovery of intrinsic unpredictabilities in nature, first at the subatomic level of quantum theory and later at the everyday level of chaos theory, showed that the physical world is something much more subtle and interesting than just a gigantic piece of clockwork. It is also perfectly possible to believe that it is more supple. Taking science seriously does not force us to an implausible denial of our basic experience of being able to exercise intentional agency. The unpredictabilities of nature can be interpreted as signifying an openness to the action of causal principles that goes beyond the reductionist picture of simply an exchange of energy between constituents. The latter is important, but it has not been demonstrated to be the whole story.

Further insight into the issue has been provided by a significant scientific development that is at present in its infancy but will surely lead to much deeper understanding. It has become possible to a modest degree to study complex systems in their entirety rather than breaking them down into component bits and pieces. This type of study reveals some surprising phenomena. For example, systems routinely display an ability to self-organize spontaneously into elaborate patterns of future total behavior, in a manner that is quite unforeseeable if one thinks solely about the character of the separate constituents. Why this happens is currently not well understood, but the emergence of these creative behavioral patterns encourages the idea that there are holistic laws of nature, at present unknown to us, for which the key concept will not be energy but something that one might call "active information," a principle that generates complex patterns in the future behavior of the whole system. We discuss this in more detail in appendix B.

These developments are very promising and suggestive, though there is much more work to be done. The dualities of parts/wholes and energy/information bear some analogical relation to the much more profound and perplexing dualities of material/mental and brain/mind. Yet there is the promise of being able to gain a degree of deeper understanding. This would be a real gain for *science* as it begins to describe a world sufficiently rich and flexible in its character for us to recognize ourselves as being among its inhabitants.

Another relevant scientific development is that of current progress in neuroscience. It has proved possible to identify many of the neural pathways by which our brains process the information that comes to us through our senses. Of course, one expects identifiable neural correlates to perception in embodied beings, and their existence by no means implies that we are nothing but complex aggregates of molecules. There is a vast, yawning gap, which no one currently knows how to bridge, between talk of neural firings, however sophisticated and interesting that may be, and the simplest of mental experiences, such as seeing red or feeling hungry. The problem of qualia (feelings) is a hard problem indeed. The talk of consciousness as "the last frontier" that the heroic armies of science are just about to cross is ill-judged and bombastic. In fact, it is possible that consciousness will never be fully understandable by scientific methods. Pretty well everything else that science investigates, from atoms to life, can be treated as external and approached from outside of itself. That is not true of consciousness, which is intrinsically private and internal. I have no direct access to any consciousness other than my own. I do not know, for example, if you experience red the same way that I do.

3. The Existence of God

Do you believe that God has made the evidence for his existence self-evident? If God is self-evident, what do you think are the most compelling self-evident arguments for his existence?

The Creator has not filled creation with items stamped "made by God." God's existence is not self-evident in some totally unambiguous and undeniable way. The presence of God is veiled because, when you think about it, the naked presence of divinity would overwhelm finite creatures, depriving them of the possibility of truly being themselves and freely accepting God. A recurring theme in this book is that, out of love, God has self-limited the exercise of divine power to give creatures the space to be themselves and, as we shall discuss when we come later to evolution, even to "make themselves." This does not mean that there are no signs of the will of the Creator or motivations to believe in God's existence but that we have to look a little below the surface of things to find them.

Interestingly enough, science is some real help to us here. While science is competent to answer its own questions, questions arise from our experience of doing science whose answering take us beyond its narrow confines. One of these is very simple but well worth thinking about: Why is science possible at all? Of course, we have to be able to understand the everyday world in order to survive in it, but why are we able also to understand the subatomic quantum world and the vast universe of cosmic, curved space-time? These domains are far from having direct impacts on our daily lives, and their understanding has called for ways of thinking that are quite different from our normal habits. (In the cloudy quantum world, if you know where something is, you can't know what it is doing, and if you know what it is doing, you can't know where it is. We cannot picture such a world, but it turns out that we can understand it to a large extent.) Not only is the universe rationally transparent to science, but it also turns out to be rationally beautiful. Fundamental physics is always expressed in terms of what mathematicians recognize to be "beautiful equations." A frequent and rewarding scientific experience is that of wonder at the beautiful patterns of order revealed to our inquiry. Science does not explain these marvelous facts. It is simply happy to exploit the opportunities that they offer. Yet the rational transparency and beauty of the universe are surely too remarkable to be treated as just happy accidents. Belief in God can make all this intelligible, for it sees the deep order of the world—a world shot through with signs of mind, one might say—as being indeed a reflection of the truth that the mind of the Creator is revealed in this way. Science is then understood to be possible because the universe is a creation and we are creatures made in the image of the Creator.

Another question arising from science but taking us beyond its explanatory reach is: Why is the universe so special? Scientists do not really like things to be special. They prefer the general. Our expectation was that our universe would be just a common or garden specimen of what a universe might be like. This has turned out to be far from the case. The argument is as follows:

The universe started in an extremely simple way. Following the big bang it was just an expanding ball of energy. Now, after 13.7 billion years, it is rich and complex, the home of saints and scientists. This fact in itself might suggest that something significant has been going on in cosmic history. But there is much more to say. As we have come to understand many of the processes by which this great fertility has come about, we have come to see that their possibility had to be built into the given physical fabric of the world from the start. The laws of physics (which science assumes but does not explain) had to take a very precise, "finely tuned" form if anything as complex as carbon-based life was to be possible. For example, the only place in the universe where carbon is made is in the nuclear furnaces of the stars. Every atom of carbon in our bodies was once inside a star—we are literally people of stardust. The process by which this happens is delicate, and if the laws of nuclear physics had been even a little bit different, there would have been no carbon, and thus no you and me. Many more examples of such fine-tuning have been identified. What are we to make of them? It would be far too intellectually lazy just to say it was all a happy accident. So remarkable a fact surely calls for an adequate explanation. Some scientists have suggested that there are trillions of different universes, all different and all separate from one another. If there were such a vast multiverse, then maybe one of those universes might by chance be suitable for carbon-based life—a kind of winning ticket in a multiversal lottery, you might say—and that, of course, would be ours since we are carbon-based life. Such a prodigal suggestion is not science, since we have no knowledge of, or access to, any universe other than our own. The multiverse is a metaphysical guess. A much more economic suggestion is that there is only one universe that is the way it is, in its fine-tuned fruitfulness, precisely because it is not just "any old world" but a creation endowed by its Creator with the potentialities that have given it so remarkable a history.

Moving away from science, there are further indications of the veiled presence of God if we are prepared to look for them. We have moral knowledge that assures us that love is better than hate, truth is better than the lie. Where does this come from? The religious person can understand our ethical intuitions to be intimations of God's good and perfect will. Similarly our aesthetic experience of encounter with deep beauty can be understood as a sharing in the Creator's joy in creation. There is widespread human testimony to a meeting with a dimension of reality that can only be described as an encounter with the sacred. There are the particular records of unique events, preserved in the faith traditions, that have been understood as moments of divine self-disclosure. On our Web site, Nicholas answered this question with a single word: "Jesus."

There are no knock-down arguments for the existence of God—or, for that matter, for divine nonexistence—in the sense that it would be completely irrational to deny them. The question is too deep for a 2 + 2 = 4 kind of proof response. Yet there are good motivations for belief in God, sufficient for many of us to commit ourselves to betting our lives on them. The claim is not that atheists are stupid, for that is clearly not the case, but that theism explains more than atheism ever could, making intelligible what otherwise would have to be treated as merely a happy accident.

4. Creation and Evolution

Does God act directly through evolution, or simply conceive the process and allow it to happen? Was God aware that it would culminate in human beings?

There is a false story, often conveyed in the media, that in 1859, when Charles Darwin published *The Origin of Species,* all the religious people opposed his ideas. This was certainly not the case. In fact, the clergyman and novelist Charles Kingsley welcomed Darwin's insights and saw how they cast new light on the doctrine of creation. Kingsley said that no doubt God could have snapped the divine fingers and brought into being a ready-made world, but it had turned out that God had chosen to do something cleverer than that, for in bringing into being an evolving world God had made a creation in which "creatures could make themselves." An important theological insight is expressed in that phrase.

The creation of the God whose nature is love will not be a kind of cosmic puppet theater in which the divine Puppet-Master pulls every string. The gift of love is always the gift of some due form of independence granted to the beloved. The creation has been endowed with great potentiality (remember fine-tuning), but the manner in which that potentiality is brought to birth in particular ways is through the shuffling explorations of the evolutionary process. The history of the universe is not the performance of a fixed score, written by God in eternity and inexorably performed by creatures, but it is a grand improvisation in which the Creator and creatures cooperate in the unfolding development of the grand fugue of creation. God is not a mere spectator of this process (we shall discuss the question of divine action later), but neither are creatures caught up willy-nilly in a process in which they have no active part to play.

We do not need to believe that *Homo sapiens,* in all our five-fingered specificity, was decreed from all eternity, but we can certainly believe that the eventual emergence of self-conscious, God-conscious beings is no accident but rather the fulfillment of the Creator's purpose. God can bring about determinate ends, even if they are achieved along contingent paths. There is a metaphor that may be helpful here, even if like all such pictures it is not perfect in every detail. The image is that of the history of creation as a game of cosmic chess, with God the Grand Master and creatures the club players. The club players are free to make whatever moves they like, but the Grand Master will win the game in the end because he understands it in the deep way that enables him to bring about his intended purpose.

5. Evil and Suffering

Was the tsunami an act of God?

The greatest difficulty for religious belief is the evil and suffering that are present in the world. This is particularly acute in relation to natural evil, the disease and disaster that are so widespread, exemplified by an event like the Indonesian tsunami of 2004. We can get some understanding of moral evil (the cruelties and neglects of humankind) as being the consequences of the abuse of the gift of free will, but surely natural evil is the responsibility of the Creator alone. This perplexity no doubt holds many back from religious belief, and it continues to trouble those of us who are believers. It would be foolish to suppose that there is some simple, one-line response to so deep a mystery, but there are some things that can be said, and science helps us to some degree in tackling the problem.

A creation in which creatures make themselves can rightly be seen as a greater good than a ready-made world would have been, but it has a necessary cost. There is an inescapable shadow side to the evolutionary process. It will yield not only great fruitfulness, but there will also necessarily be ragged edges and blind alleys. The engine that has driven the development of life on Earth has been genetic mutation. But if the DNA in germ cells is able to mutate and produce new forms of life, the DNA of somatic cells will also be able to mutate, and when that happens, it may produce malignancy. The presence of cancer in the world is undoubtedly an anguishing fact, but it is not simply gratuitous, something that a Creator who was a bit more competent or a bit less callous could easily have eliminated. It is the shadow side of a world in which creatures can make themselves. We all tend to think that had we been in charge of creation, frankly we would have done it better. We would have kept all the nice things (flowers and sunsets) and got rid of all the nasty ones (disease and disaster). Science shows us that this is just not possible. The processes of the world are so intricately intertwined that one cannot separate the good from the bad, keeping the one and discarding the other. It is a package deal.

This insight does not remove all our perplexity, but it is of some help. It applies to the tsunami. Earthquakes occur, and if they are under the sea they generate tsunamis, because there are tectonic plates that sometimes slip. Would it not have been better, therefore, for God to arrange for the earth to have a solid crust all over? The answer is, No, it wouldn't. The gaps between the plates enable mineral resources to well up from deeper down and replenish the face of the earth. Without this happening, life would not be able to keep going very long.

Was the tsunami an act of God? God certainly allowed it to happen in a creation that is given its freedom to be and to make itself, but God did not will it as some terrible kind of punishment.

6. Divine Action

A number of questions have related to John Polkinghorne's ideas about how God might interact with the history of creation. This is a key issue for a theology in which God is neither a kind of cosmic tyrant, determining everything and giving creatures no real freedom, nor a deistic spectator, who set it all going and then simply stands back to watch what happens. The issues are complicated and not susceptible to being encapsulated in a concise quotation from an inquirer. The response will therefore have to start by going into some detail, explaining what are the problems involved.

In the past, science had seen all causality in terms of the exchange of energy. But the discovery of intrinsic unpredictabilities in nature is a sign that the world is open to the action of new causal principles. As we suggested in our response to question 2, one of these principles could be what we call "active information." This offers the prospect of beginning to understand how human beings are able to exercise intentional agency. If we can play our minor roles in contributing to the future of an open world, it would scarcely be surprising if that world's Creator had retained some providential power to influence the shape of the future also. This could be pictured as being due to the divine input of pure (i.e., unembodied) information into the open history of creation.

It's time to take a closer look at this proposal. The first thing to note is that though science constrains our thinking about causality, it does not wholly determine the form that thinking should take. Doing that requires making a metaphysical decision that goes beyond what science itself can say. Consider quantum physics. Most people think that quantum theory is probabilistic and indeterministic. The first statement is certainly true. Quantum theory can say that there is a 50 per cent chance that a radioactive nucleus will decay in the next hour, but it cannot say whether any particular nucleus will actually do so. However, the second statement is not necessarily true. Conventional quantum theory, pioneered by Niels Bohr and his successors, certainly holds that the probabilities of the theory arise from an intrinsic indeterminacy present in its processes. However, David Bohm produced an alternative interpretation in which the probabilities arise simply from ignorance about the details of what is a deterministic process. These two interpretations yield precisely the same predictions for experimental results, so scientific investigation cannot decide between them. The choice between Bohr or Bohm has to be made on other, that is to say, metaphysical, grounds.

The need for this choice results from an important philosophical distinction between epistemology and ontology. Epistemology is concerned with what we can know; ontology is concerned with what is actually the case. The two are not necessarily the same, and there is room for philosophical choice and argument about what kind of relationship shall be assumed. How things appear to us might be different from the way they actually are in their true selves. Quantum theory may look indeterministic, but this could be because of a necessary ignorance of all the factors involved rather than the presence of an absolute indeterminacy.

The philosophical stance that seeks to align epistemology and ontology as closely as possible is called realism. Scientists are instinctively realists. They believe that what we know should be taken to be a reliable guide to what is the case. It is difficult to see why one should go to all the trouble involved in scientific research if one did not believe that it was telling us what the world is actually like. Unpredictability is a kind of epistemological deficit. We cannot know beforehand what the future behavior is going to be. It is perfectly natural for a realist to interpret unpredictabilities as also being signs of an ontological openness, a stance that is highly persuasive if it offers the opportunity to begin to accommodate our basic human experiences of acting as intentional agents. Similarly, the religious person is free to believe in the exercise of divine providential action within history while taking with absolute seriousness all that science can truly tell us about the way the world works.

A correspondent to the Web site wrote, "It seems to me that Polkinghorne's theory [of divine action] is vulnerable to the assertion that the epistemologically indeterminate does not equal the ontologically indeterminate." We can agree that *logically* the two are not necessarily the same, but we can assert the perfectly proper right to opt for the metaphysical realist position of choosing to align them, thereby gaining a valuable insight into the exercise of human agency and divine providence.

7. Jesus Christ

What can people believe and still be Christians? All that was necessary was for the disciples to believe that Jesus was resurrected, not for him actually to be resurrected. [This person goes on to suggest that the body might have been stolen from the tomb by a lone prankster.] [As a historian] I know better than most how flimsy the evidence surrounding Christ actually is.

Remarks of this kind raise the vital question of what we can actually know about Jesus of Nazareth and how we should think about him. Scientists are instinctively what one may call "bottom-up thinkers," seeking always to move from evidence to interpretation and then on to motivated belief. Because the physical world has proved surprising, far beyond our powers of prior expectation (think of quantum theory), the natural question for a scientist to ask about a proposed belief is not "Is it reasonable?"—as if we knew beforehand the shape that reason had to take—but "What makes you think that might be the case?" Addressing Christian belief in this spirit requires careful consideration of what is actually known about Jesus.

There is a vast literature on the topic, presenting many different and contradictory points of view, and it is not possible in the space available here to deal with it at all adequately. John devoted a substantial fraction of *The Faith of a Physicist* to discussing the issue. Here we can only offer two leading thoughts.

The first is to deny that the evidence about Christ is "flimsy." The earliest Christian writings are the epistles of St. Paul, with the Gospels coming later. The first Gospel, Mark, was probably written about thirty-five to forty years after the events it describes, but all these early writings incorporate material that scholars believe predates them, some of it coming very close to the time of Jesus himself. Remember also that first-century Palestine was a culture with a strong oral tradition, skilled at preserving and handing on significant accounts. There are many scholarly estimates seeking a careful and scrupulous evaluation of the evidence about Christ. Of course, there are disagreements about the conclusions to be reached, but books such as those by Richard Bauckham, J. D. G. Dunn, L. Hurtado, E. P. Sanders, and N. T. Wright[1] present powerful cases for the essential reliability of the accounts given. The evidence for the character, words, and deeds of Jesus deserves serious consideration by any honest inquirer.

The second thought is to note a striking difference between Jesus and other great founders of world religions, such as Moses, the Buddha, and Mohammed. All the religious leaders have many things in common. All say wise things; all are credited with remarkable deeds; all have a charismatic power to draw and influence their followers. But Jesus is different in a striking way.

The others all end their lives in honored old age, surrounded by faithful disciples who are resolved to carry on the work and message of the Master. Jesus dies in mid-life, deserted by his followers, suffering a painful and shameful death that any first-century Jew would see as a sign of God's rejection (Deuteronomy says, "Cursed is anyone hung on a tree") and with a cry of dereliction on his lips: "My God, my God, why have you forsaken me?" On the face of it, however promising Jesus' public ministry may have appeared to have been, in the end it all seems to have ended in failure and disillusionment. If that had been the case, and the story of Jesus ended completely at that grim place of crucifixion, it seems highly likely that he would just have disappeared from history. Yet we have all heard of Jesus. Something happened to continue his story. The writers of the New Testament all tell us that it was his resurrection by God on the third day, to live an unending new life of lordship and glory. Can we possibly believe them?

The significance of Jesus turns on the question of the resurrection. If indeed he was raised from death, never to die again, then there is surely something uniquely significant about him. The New Testament offers two lines of evidence for its remarkable claim of resurrection: the stories of the appearances of the risen Christ and the stories of the finding of the empty tomb. The assessment of these stories calls for much careful consideration. We suggest two of the many reasons for taking the task seriously. The appearance stories are varied in type and location in the different Gospels, but there is a common feature: on each occasion it was initially difficult to recognize who was present. Mary Magdalene thought it was a gardener; the couple on the road to Emmaus had no notion until the end of the journey who their companion was; and so on. This seems strange if what is involved is just a gaggle of independently made-up stories. Might it not be an actual historical reminiscence of the character of the encounters? As for the discovery of the empty tomb, why make women (considered unreliable witnesses in the ancient world) the discoverers, unless they actually were?

We have only been able to touch on a tiny part of a vast and important topic, but perhaps enough has been said to indicate that Christianity has reasons to claim that it shares in the great search for truth, attainable through motivated belief.

8. Final Destiny

Besides Jesus' resurrection, on what basis does John Polkinghorne develop his eschatology and general views about the world to come?

We can start with something Jesus said when he had an argument with the Sadducees about whether there is a destiny beyond death (Mark 12:18–27). He pointed them to the God of Abraham, Isaac, and Jacob and commented, "'He is not God of the dead, but of the living.'" The point is a powerful one. If the patriarchs mattered to God once, as they certainly did, then they must matter to the faithful God forever. They will not be cast aside at their deaths as if they were broken pots that had served their purpose and could now be discarded. Their life continues. The same will be true of us. There is no natural hope of a destiny beyond death, a story that science could tell us in terms of its "horizontal" account of what happens now. But that is not the only story to be told. Religion can tell the "vertical" story of God's faithfulness, and that story undergirds the hope, already manifested by Jesus' resurrection, that the last word does not lie with death but with God.

If we try to think what a life beyond this one might be like, we immediately face the problem that there has to be both continuity and discontinuity involved. The continuity arises because it really must be Abraham, Isaac, and Jacob who live again and not just new persons given the old names for old times' sake. The carrier of continuity between life in this world and life in the world to come has usually been seen to be the human soul. In response to question 2, we rejected the idea of the soul as a detachable spiritual component. If we accept that we are psychosomatic unities, the idea of the soul will have to be reconceptualized. Whatever it is, it is surely "the real me," carrying continuity in this life as much as beyond it. What makes an elderly person the same as the young schoolboy in the photograph of sixty years ago? It is tempting to say that it is material continuity, but that is actually an illusion. The atoms that make up our bodies are changing all the time, through wear and tear, eating and drinking. What gives continuity are not the atoms themselves but the almost infinitely complex information-bearing pattern in which they are organized. The essence of this pattern is the soul. It will dissolve at death with the decay of the body, but it is a perfectly coherent belief that the faithful God will not allow it to be lost but will preserve it in the divine memory. That in itself would not be the continuance of human life beyond death, for it is intrinsic to human beings that we are embodied in some way. We are not apprentice angels but men and women. Thus the ultimate Christian hope is resurrection, God's great eschatological act of the reimbodiment of information-bearing pattern in the environment of the new creation.

This brings in the theme of discontinuity. The patriarchs will not be made alive again simply in order to die again. The "matter" of the new creation, making up their resurrected bodies, must be different from the matter of this world. Death is present in this world because of the second law of thermodynamics, which says that in the end, disorder always wins over order. However, it seems perfectly coherent to believe that God could bring into being a new kind of "matter" with such strong self-organizing principles that the drift to disorder would no longer happen. If so, why did God not do so in the first place? The answer lies in the fact that creation by the God of love has to be a two-stage process. First, there is old creation, existing at some distance from the veiled presence of its Creator, necessary if finite creatures are to be able to make a truly free response without being overwhelmed by the Infinite. This is the world in which creatures are allowed to make themselves, and the evolutionary process necessarily involves the presence of death as one generation has to give way to the new life of the next. God's final intention, however, is the new creation, drawn freely into such close connection with its Creator that its "matter," suffused with the direct presence of a God no longer veiled, will permit the everlasting processes of eternal life.

Present thought about the nature of our destiny beyond death necessarily involves a degree of speculation. At some point, the best response is simply to say, "Wait and see," something the Christian can do with confidence in the faithfulness of the God and Father of our Lord Jesus Christ.

9. Atheism

In response to Richard Dawkins's polemical emphasis on the dark side of religion shown by crusades and inquisitions, we drew attention to the terrible acts of the atheist regimes of Stalin, Hitler, and Pol Pot. A contributor rebuked us for "suggesting that their horrific activities were somehow inspired by their lack of belief in a God."

Both religious and nonreligious communities have been responsible for deeds for which one can only feel penitence and shame. The principal point of our response was to counter a false polemic implying that these sorts of terrible events were primarily induced by religion. In fact, they arise from a distortion present in human nature itself, the slantedness that so often turns a country's liberator into its next tyrant. The Christian diagnosis of this condition is that it arises from sin, by which is meant an alienation from God. Human life will only find its true fulfillment when it is lived in communion with the One who is the source of our being. To say that is by no means to deny the plain fact that many atheists are people of moral conviction and ethical intentions. There are many problems facing humanity whose tackling requires the utmost cooperation between people of good will and concern for the common good, both religious and nonreligious.

Further Studies

Some books covering the general field of science and religion are the following:

Alexander, Denis. 2001. *Rebuilding the Matrix: Science and Faith in the 21st Century*. Oxford: Lion.

Barbour, I. G. 1998. *Religion and Science: Historical and Contemporary Issues.* London: SCM Press.

Peacocke, Arthur. 1993. *Theology for a Scientific Age: Being and Becoming—Natural, Divine and Human.* Enlarg. ed. Minneapolis: Augsburg.

Polkinghorne, John. 1998. *Science and Theology: An Introduction.* London: SPCK.

2

The Concept and Existence of God

10. Can God's Existence Be Proved?

If a proof of God's existence can be made, then how important is it? Such a proof could meet scientific standards, such as being falsifiable, and precisely define the points that are provable and when faith begins.

NB: Outside mathematics proofs can only be persuasive, never utterly conclusive. After all, God does not force us to believe; he wants faith. The faith he wants is not "blind trust, ignoring the evidence" but a relationship of belief and trust. Suppose you have found a teacher who over many years has proven to be loving and wise. Then it is rational to trust that person when he or she tells you something that he or she is in a position to know, even if you do not have other independent evidence for this.

It is also important to remember that belief in God does not, primarily, mean assent to a set of intellectual propositions,but rather belief and trust in a person.

A philosopher, a scientist, and a simpleton—none of whom could swim—were trapped in a cove with sheer cliff faces. They split up, but the tide kept coming in. Rescuers lowered a rope with a safety harness. The philosopher said, "Ah, this looks just like a rope, but I might be mistaken—it could be wishful thinking or an illusion." So he didn't attach himself, and he was drowned. The scientist said, "Ah, this is an 11 mm polyester rope with a breaking strain of 2800 kg. It conforms to the MR 10-81 standard," and then proceeded to give an exhaustive, and entirely correct, analysis of the rope's physical and chemical properties. But he didn't attach himself and was drowned. The simpleton said, "Ah, a python! I'll attach myself to its tail."

Of course, other things being equal, it is better to have an enlightened faith in God than an unenlightened faith. But mere intellectual understanding that does not lead to action is not what God is after. We should be doers of the Word, and not just hearers.

JP: Proof is a limited category, even in mathematics. Kurt Gödel showed that axiomatized systems that contain the integers cannot prove their own consistency, and if they are consistent they contain true propositions that can be stated but not proved within the system. In science, things are yet more precarious, as theory and experiment interlace in inescapable circularity (theory interprets experiments; experiments confirm or disconfirm theories). Nevertheless, we have adequate reasons for committing ourselves to scientific beliefs. (Michael Polanyi, in his book *Personal Knowledge,* is very helpful on this.) I think that religious belief is similar. Faith involves trusting in well-motivated beliefs, not shutting one's intellectual eyes and believing impossible things because some unquestionable authority told you to. I wrote my Gifford Lectures (published as *Science and Christian Belief* in the United Kingdom and *The Faith of a Physicist* in North America) to defend Christian belief exactly along these evidence-motivated lines.

11. Is God a Delusion?

Richard Dawkins's The God Delusion *seems to heavily discredit the idea of a personal God, as traditionally believed in by religious people. He claims that the concept of God, especially that of the Jewish Bible, is both immoral and irrational (from the perspective of science). As a scientist and a religious believer, what is your view on these claims?*

NB: My initial reaction was that Dawkins has been ranting about God for many years and has never taken the trouble to understand the concept. For example, the choice of the word *delusion* rather than *mistake* appears to be part of a misleading attempt to portray religious belief as some kind of mental illness. Alister McGrath had already done a reasonable job of refuting some of his bad arguments in his book *Dawkins' God.* Of course *The God Delusion* then became a publishing phenomenon, selling over 1.5 million copies. Respected preachers urged their congregation to buy the book—and I read it, and many of the reviews.

Like most of the serious reviewers, I found it a deeply disappointing book. Terry Eagleton famously compared it to a book on biology written by someone whose sole knowledge of the subject comes from having once read the *Book of British Birds.* Even great admirers of Dawkins, writing in the journals *Nature* and *Science,* damned the book with faint praise, and *Nature* ran an illustration of Dawkins as a sandwich-board man proclaiming "Renounce God and Be Saved." At no point does Dawkins seriously engage with the arguments for religion or the existence of God, and some of the points he makes are ludicrous: a shining example being the claim that "becoming a monk was the easiest way for the young Mendel to pursue his science."—Mendel became a "monk" when he was twenty-one and began his experiments thirteen years later. Alister McGrath produced a "rapid rebuttal" called *The Dawkins Delusion*, and John Cornwell an elegant riposte called *Darwin's Angel.* Other valuable book-length responses include John Crean's *A Catholic Replies to Professor Dawkins*, Keith Ward's *Why There Almost Certainly Is a God*, and Nicky Gumbel's *Is God a Delusion?* Dawkins is writing very much in popular culture: for example, his book has endorsements from a writer of children's fantasy, two writers of *PopSci*, a rock musician, and a magician. The only Christian philosophers he engages with at all are Thomas Aquinas (four references, the same number as given to Douglas Adams) and Richard Swinburne (just three), but the discussion is superficial and full of misunderstandings and errors.

He does mention "good scientists who are sincerely religious" (including John) but says that he "remains baffled by their belief in the details of the Christian religion: resurrection, forgiveness of sins and all." I hope that when he reads this book, he will be a bit less baffled—curiously neither resurrection nor forgiveness of sins appear in the index of *The God Delusion*. Also, although the resurrection is genuinely astonishing, the idea of forgiveness of sins is not so far from Dawkins's own field or experience, and it would be interesting to know why he finds this particularly problematic. He knows about evolutionary game theory and should be aware that, under wide conditions, strategies involving forgiveness (such as Generous Tit-for-Tat) outperform "selfish" strategies like Tit-for-Tat. Furthermore, a fascinating result from Nicholas's collaborators shows that even if you have the option to impose costly punishment on Defectors, it is often better not to use it. He is, of course, almost equally bemused by quantum theory—mercifully string theory doesn't even make the index. It is not an accident that thinking deeply about the fundamental nature of reality can yield a paradoxical picture that is repugnant to common sense. John's book *Quantum Physics and Theology: An Unexpected Kinship* offers a deep and insightful exploration of some of the parallels. As John Cottingham puts it in his book *The Spiritual Dimension*, "Given that we allow physicists to invoke entities whose nature they can approach only via such indirect means . . . it seems hard to deny in advance to the religious adherent any similar right to speak of a divine reality that transcends the resources of directly descriptive language."

Of course, God is not an object on which one can do experiments—God inevitably transcends science. It is easy to say that an idea is absurd when you don't understand it. But since we have no idea what constitutes the dark matter and dark energy that seem to make up over 90 percent of the universe, the idea that "nothing can be true unless it is well-understood scientifically" is ludicrous. And the idea that "you should not believe anything unless it can be scientifically proven" is self-refuting, since that statement is itself beyond science's power to prove. However, if a loving ultimate Creator exists, then God cannot be *less than* personal: one of the many reasons the doctrine of the Trinity makes so much sense is that it shows how God can be both personal and more than personal.

It is certainly true that you can find bits of the Old Testament that apparently advocate highly immoral behavior. I don't know how my Jewish friends deal with this, but for Christians all Scripture must be understood in the light of Christ, and we know that the "bloodthirsty" bits are not to be taken "literally." This is not a new "liberal" position—St Augustine took this line in the fifth century.

There is a great deal more that can be said about *The God Delusion*, and it is good that Dawkins has helped to bring discussion about God more into the forefront. I suppose that as Christian apologists we should be glad that it is such a flawed book, but these are serious issues that deserve a much better treatment. And a number of senior scientists have come to the view that by taking shrill positions that go well beyond his area of expertise, Dawkins is bringing science into disrepute. This is a serious problem, with enrollment in "hard" science courses plummeting in the United Kingdom and the United States and major scientific facilities being cut back while governments waste money on populist initiatives. It is interesting that Dawkins seems to have softened his antireligious rhetoric recently. He now describes himself as a "Cultural Christian" and an admirer of Jesus—suggesting that people should wear "Atheists for Jesus" T-shirts.

JP: I have read *The God Delusion*, and I am afraid that Nicholas is right. It is simply an atheistic rant—a disappointing book full of assertion but devoid of real engagement with theological arguments. Much of it is taken up with stories about religious people who have done terrible things or said foolish things. Of course, this has happened. But there is no honest recognition in the book of the many occasions on which religious people have done good deeds—of compassion, peacemaking, and artistic creativity—or said wise and insightful things. Nor is there adequate recognition that many nonreligious people have also done terrible things or said foolish things. Think of Hitler, Stalin, and Pol Pot.

12. How Can God Inhabit Eternity?

If the eternal time that God inhabits carries on along some sort of linear path like our time appears to us (i.e., there is a "before" and an "after" in heaven, which would appear to be the case from reading Revelation), then surely it is impossible for an infinite amount of this time to have passed prior to the beginning of our universe. Is this something to do with our perception of time? Could it be that the time of our universe sits in relation to all of eternity like a finite line superimposed onto an infinite axis? If so, does God sit at all points on this infinite axis at the same time? If so, can he create beings with free will?

NB: Since we cannot adopt a "God's eye view," the relationship between our perception of time and God's is necessarily obscure to us. The old idea that God must be eternal and hence not experience time at all used to be almost universally held in Western Christian theology, but it has been superseded, in our view, by the realization that it is more biblical to see a personal God truly engaged with other creatures in a way that respects their freedom to choose. However, before the creation of the universe there were no clocks, thus the concept of "an infinite time before" creation does not really apply.

If God creates other beings who are really free to choose to love, then he must give these beings the real possibility of choosing something that he does not want. Thus, any creation of such beings must involve the Creator limiting his inherent powers. In particular, an omnipotent being can choose not to do things and choose not to know things. It may be that God has created a universe in which whether a specific event occurs at a specific time in the future is unknowable even by him. It may equally be that God has created a universe in which he could observe future events if he wanted to but he chooses not to in order to give his creatures freedom. Both of these possibilities show how the fact that God is the Creator does not entail a lack of freedom on our part.

JP: Of course, all theists will believe that there is an eternal aspect in God, so that divine love and faithfulness are utterly unchanging. I believe, in addition, that when God created a temporal world, God graciously chose to engage with its temporal history. This is certainly the picture the Bible seems to give when it speaks of God's involvement with the unfolding history of the chosen people, Israel, and the coming of God's Son in the first-century life of Jesus Christ. Those who think this way have a dipolar picture of the divine nature as having both eternal and temporal aspects.

13. Does God Know Everything?

Thinking of time as a dimension, I imagine it unfolded, from God's perspective, in an instant at the moment of creation. We are experiencing only the present moment, and, similarly, only the part of the universe near us that our senses can perceive. But God sees it all at once. I wonder if you could briefly explain why you find it necessary that God should limit his omniscience in order that we have free will.

NB: What I think we can say clearly is that if it is necessary for God to limit his omniscience in order that we might have free will, then he will have done so (see our response to question 19).

The basic problem is whether time is inherently linear or branching. If it is "fixed" whether or not Al will marry Bet on 1 July 2010, then Al and Bet have no choice in the matter and therefore, on most natural interpretations of free will, no free will about it. There are philosophers who try to argue that free will is compatible with determinism, but I don't find their arguments at all convincing.

It would seem that, from a "God's eye view," future events must be "fixed," because even if no human knows what will happen, God does. But this only works if we interpret omniscience in terms of "knowing everything that can be known" rather than "knowing anything that can be known if you choose to do so," and indeed only the second definition is compatible with God's omnipotence (because otherwise God would be unable to choose not to know something).

We now understand in basic physics that the very act of observing something necessarily changes the outcome. Still, nobody really knows how time appears to God, and it may well be that these speculations are hilariously misconceived from God's point of view. All we can know for certain is that the reality will be more wonderful and infused with love than our conception, and that God, having labored mightily so that we can be free to choose to love, will not have carelessly undermined the whole enterprise.

JP: My argument is not that God's not knowing the future is essential to guarantee free will, but that a world that can contain freely choosing beings must be open to the future so that it is a world of true becoming. The argument then is that God will know that world truly, that is, according to its actual nature in its actual becomingness. The consequence is a divine choice to engage with time and not know the details of the future. This seems to me very much the way the Bible speaks about God's chosen relationship with creatures. Nevertheless, these matters are contentious and our understanding limited. The view of God's knowing the whole of temporal history "all at once" has had many supporters, including Augustine and Aquinas, so you are in good company. They believe this idea was consistent with human free will since it did not involve *fore*knowledge of an event—all events are contemporary to the divine atemporal gaze.

14. Is Everything Divinely Predestined?

I noticed that John Polkinghorne talked of destiny and predestination in one of his books. But how can the universe be free when Paul himself speaks of predestination (Rom. 8)?

NB & JP: The Bible only uses the word "predestination" twice, in one passage, and what Paul means there is that it is God's intention from the beginning of time that we should be saved through Jesus, and that it is God who calls, justifies, and glorifies. It is not through any merit of our own. Paul is not taking a scientific or philosophical position on whether the future is predetermined. The Bible speaks of love all the time, in every book of the New Testament and most of the books in the Old. Love is central to Paul's theology, and indeed to the theology of the New Testament.

One of the major advances in theology and philosophy over the last fifty years is a deeper understanding of the connection between love and freedom. Alongside this we are able to glimpse the sheer brilliance of God's creation in solving an apparently impossible problem: How can an omnipotent and omniscient God create beings that are genuinely free to choose to love? The answer seems to be by creating a universe that has *just* the right balance between lawfulness and randomness to allow free-will beings to evolve (see our responses to questions 19 and 20).

The American psychologist William James liked to speak of the Creator as a Chess Grand Master engaged in a game with club-player opponents. The Grand Master will win the game, whatever moves the players freely make. In other words, we can believe that God will bring about his purposed ends by contingent means, while always respecting our free will in his generous and perfect love.

15. Is God the Source of All Morality?

I wonder what John Polkinghorne thinks of the Euthyphro dilemma? The dilemma simply stated suggests that either (a) God is the very source of all morality, in which case we are forced to concede that good and evil are simply arbitrary things that God chooses to condone and condemn respectively; or (b) morality exists on a more fundamental level than God, in which case we are forced to concede that God is not the source of all morality and that, presumably, there are certain things he cannot do (i.e., those things that have been defined to be evil without reference to God). Is this a problem for Christians? Or is this simply a false dilemma in that there are more than two possible options and we have just been presented with two that suit the argument?

NB: As far as I can see, from a philosophical point of view Christianity is the claim ("Jesus is Lord") that the ultimate Creator (God) has the essential nature of Jesus. (UC ≡ J if you like symbols.) We know from his words and actions that Jesus' essential nature is loving—from which it follows easily that God's essential nature is loving ("God is Love"). If you love someone, you steadfastly will their ultimate good. It thus follows that it is part of God's essential nature that his commands will be for our ultimate good. This is therefore not a dilemma for Christianity, although it is for abstract theism.

JP: The classic Christian answer, made by thinkers such as Thomas Aquinas, is to speak of the simple unity of the divine Being, for whom essence and existence, goodness and will, are identical and not to be divided from each other. God's being almighty does not mean God can do anything whatsoever, however arbitrary, but rather anything that is in accord with the divine nature and will. God is not limited from the outside but internally self-constrained by divine consistency.

16. What about the Trinity?

NB & JP: People are sometimes bemused that scientifically literate Christians believe in the Trinity. It is not difficult, by quoting some phrases from one of the historic creeds ("Yet there are not three incomprehensibles, but one incomprehensible"), to make the whole idea sound like mumbo jumbo. And all Christians agree that the Trinity is a mystery.

Any deep understanding of the fundamental nature of reality is bound to be something of a mystery. Theologians arrived at the doctrine of the Trinity after long and careful reflection on the facts that they observed, in a rather similar way to how physicists arrived at the Standard Model after sixty years of reflection on a whole series of remarkable discoveries and theoretical insights and a great many blind alleys.

From the "fundamental equation" of Christianity (UC ≡ J) it follows that authentic records of the life of Jesus and its immediate aftermath are of immense value and need to be taken very seriously—they are analogous to the data coming from the cosmic background radiation, which give us details of the big bang. It also follows that essentially authentic records will exist—an ultimate Creator can hardly be incompetent. So the question naturally arises, What is the relationship between the ultimate Creator and Jesus? To the fiercely monotheistic Jews who were Jesus' first disciples, the idea that there was more than one God was utterly unacceptable: almost everyone else in their world believed in a whole series of gods, but they held to their belief in one God, to the death. Yet Jesus says, "I and the Father are one," and when Thomas addresses him as "my Lord and my God," he does not correct him.

While they were puzzling over this, another puzzle, even harder for us to grasp, was deeply urgent. Christians experienced the presence of what they called, and still call, the Holy Spirit. The idea of the Spirit of God was familiar from the Old Testament, but there it seemed to be referring to a mode of God's presence. However, Jesus speaks of the Holy Spirit as an equal, and when Christians first experienced the Holy Spirit, they sometimes talked of "the Spirit of Jesus" as if "Spirit of God," "Spirit of Jesus," and "Holy Spirit" are interchangeable terms.

Again, this is not unlike the situation that the pioneers of quantum theory faced: as they did increasingly careful experiments, things that they "knew" to be particles behaved like waves, and things they knew to be waves behaved like particles.

As they developed the theory, highly paradoxical effects were predicted, such as quantum entanglement, which ran counter to much of what was considered certain. How *could* a measurement of the state of one particle instantly "force" another particle to be in a different state? Yet careful reflection on increasingly careful experiments showed that it was so.

This is not the place to discuss in detail either the reasons behind the doctrine of the Trinity (John's *Science and the Trinity* would be a good place to start) or the parallels explored in John's *Quantum Physics and Theology*. In the end, in formulating the doctrine of the Trinity, pretty well the simplest and most symmetrical model that fits the observations turns out to be the correct one—as far as the official theology of at least 90 percent of Christians is concerned: that the Father, the Son, and the Holy Spirit are all God but in such perfect loving unity that there are not three Gods but one God. As always with a deep theory it makes sense of many other puzzles: not least by placing love right at the heart of the Godhead, since it doesn't make much sense to speak of love without a beloved and simply to love your self is not the highest form of love.

To a twenty-first-century scientist, the idea that love should be at the center of the deepest understanding of the universe is perhaps not as surprising as it would be to someone with an earlier scientific worldview. The theme of cooperation runs so deep in biology that it has been suggested that cooperation should be seen as one of the basic principles of evolution (see appendix C). And it is no accident that St. Paul uses a biological metaphor in the cooperation of different parts of the body to illustrate the qualities of unselfish love that he sees as essential for Christians.

But like any truly deep theory, there is also a mystery. It has been said that anyone who thinks he or she fully understands quantum mechanics doesn't understand it at all, and it has been proven that no rich logical theory can be complete and consistent. Thus to an even greater extent any true statements about the nature of an ultimate Creator must transcend the limits of human language and human understanding. Even after a lifetime of the closest association, however well or intimately you know someone, you can never completely know another human being. Still less can we completely know the extraordinary transcendent community of perfect love, wisdom, and creativity that Christians believe lies at the heart of reality.

Further Studies

Davies, Paul. 1992. *The Mind of God: The Scientific Basis for a Rational World.* New York: Touchstone.

Plantinga, Alvin. 1990. *God and Other Minds: A Study of the Rational Justification of Belief in God.* Ithaca, NY: Cornell University Press.

Polkinghorne, John. 1998. *Belief in God in an Age of Science.* New Haven, CT: Yale University Press.

Russell, Robert John, William R. Stoeger, and George V. Coyne, eds. 1988. *Physics, Philosophy, and Theology: A Common Quest for Understanding.* Vatican City: Vatican Observatory.

Swinburne, Richard. 1993. *The Coherence of Theism.* Oxford: Oxford University Press.

3
The Universe

17. How Did the Universe Begin?

I am currently reading a debate (book) between William Lane Craig and Sinnett-Armstrong. Craig is of course up with the Kalam cosmological argument on the premise "everything that begins to exist has a cause." However, Sinnett-Armstrong claims that one interpretation of quantum physics says that particles can in fact come out of nothing. If that is the case, could the universe have popped out of nothing?

NB & JP: Arguments for the existence of God may be persuasive, but like all nonmathematical arguments that use inductive methods, such as those used in science, history, and ordinary life, they can never be conclusive in the sense that the premises of an inductive argument do not logically entail its conclusion. Besides, one can always dispute the premises of an argument, whether it is deductive or inductive. It is certainly possible to formulate the Kalam cosmological argument so that it is formally valid (i.e., the conclusions do follow from the premises), and it probably does show that *either* the universe was caused by an ultimate Creator *or* there is an infinite regress of causes *or* the universe is ultimately un-caused.

Current versions of quantum theory do indeed allow for the spontaneous emergence of particles from the quantum vacuum. But the quantum vacuum is not "nothing" in any sensible philosophical sense. It is more like a field of energy that pervades the whole universe.

But the current understanding of cosmology is surely not the last word. It is now known that only 4 percent of the matter and energy in the universe is made of what we understand as matter, and most of the universe seems, on current understandings, to be "dark matter" (22 percent) and "dark energy" (74 percent) about which we know very little. In addition, no one knows how to reconcile quantum mechanics with general relativity. The string theory has certainly inspired some elegant and deep mathematics, but it looks increasingly unlikely that it will yield good new physics without some fundamental new insights, and many of the speculations that have emerged from it have a rather desperate feel. It could be, in the words of Peter Woit's book, *Not Even Wrong*.

In quantum theory the vacuum is the state of lowest energy, but it is not a state of nonactivity. The reason lies in Heisenberg's uncertainty principle. To see the point in an uncomplicated way, think about the simple model of a pendulum. In Newtonian mechanics, its lowest energy state is with the bob at rest at the bottom. Heisenberg does not agree with this conclusion, for you would know both the position of the bob (at the bottom) and also its momentum (zero). A quantum pendulum has always to be quivering a little (vacuum fluctuations). Particles can emerge out of and disappear into this active vacuum, but it is clearly not "nothing." The quantum vacuum is not a "free lunch" as people sometimes say, but its cost is the laws of quantum mechanics themselves. The theist will see these as expressions of the Creator's will.

18. How Can Something Come from Nothing?

How can we say that in the beginning there was nothing and then there was something when there was nothing from which the something could come from? It seems impossible for the big bang to hap-

pen without the aid of God. There was not even the potential for the big bang before it was said to be made actual; it is simply a logically impossible supposition that something can explode out of nothing.

NB: There are certainly grave difficulties for atheists in the big bang, which is one reason why it was resisted for so long. Indeed the term "big bang" was applied to this idea by Fred Hoyle in an effort to discredit it—it looked far too much like creation (and it probably didn't help that this set of solutions to the Einstein equation was discovered by a Catholic priest). Atheists tend to reply that you have to assume something—why not that (or the laws of nature/ the quantum vacuum/an infinite series of big bangs, etc.)?

It is, perhaps, conceivable that the quantum vacuum just exists, with no explanation, and is the fundamental entity on which the universe is based. But if this were true, it would be a very surprising additional fact—it is perfectly conceivable that the quantum vacuum was caused by some other more fundamental entity. Indeed when it suits them, atheist scientists are quite prepared to discuss "pre-big-bang cosmologies." But there is a long tradition in atheist philosophy, as in politics, of saying, "There is no answer to this question" when what you mean is "There is an answer to this question, but I don't like it."

JP: Certainly the quantum vacuum is not "nothing"; it is a structured and highly active entity. Science does not offer the universe as a "free lunch," as some allege, but the cost of the cosmic meal is the laws of quantum theory and relativity, graciously provided by the Creator. Every metaphysical scheme has to have its unexplained foundation, for in philosophy nothing comes of nothing. The materialist takes as basic fact the existence of matter. The theist takes as basic fact the existence of a divine creator.

19. Isn't Everything Random?

I am continually hearing that the fact that the subatomic world is random shows that God did not create it. My question is, "What effect would a structured or organized subatomic world have on cre-

ation?" As water has unique properties that are necessary, could it be that a random subatomic world is what makes creation possible?

NB: First of all, the word "random" is somewhat slippery and hard to define. In the context of quantum mechanics, we can take it as meaning "there is no physical way to predict with certainty the outcome of an observation (where quantum effects are appreciable)." This of course does not say that there may not be other, nonscientific factors at work in influencing the actual outcomes. So it is perfectly possible that God might "fix" the outcomes of these uncertain observations in such a way as to conform with the overall probabilities given by the laws of physics. However, the idea that God tinkers with reality to hide the true nature of the world seems highly implausible, and we are much more inclined to believe that the indeterminacy of the fundamental physical laws reflects a deep fact about the nature of the universe: that God has created it with real freedom inherent in the deepest level of creation. This seems to be part of God's answer to the seemingly insoluble problem of "How can an omnipotent Creator create a universe in which beings are free to choose to love him and each other?"

It is fair to mention that although the observations from measurements are probabilistic, the wave function (which represents the state of a quantum-mechanical system) develops over time according to the Dirac equation, which is deterministic. This is one of the factors that leads to the notorious "measurement problem" of quantum mechanics, to which there is no agreed philosophical or scientific answer (Roger Penrose, for example, has a conjecture that it involves gravity). John and I, and most working scientists, favor the "Copenhagen Interpretation," which essentially accepts that, in some poorly understood way, a "measurement" is a fundamental "operation" that forces the wave function to "choose" which state it falls into. However the "many worlds" interpretation, which suggests that there are an unbounded number of other universes in which the measurements just come out differently, has a growing number of adherents—it seems to appeal particularly (though by no means exclusively!) to atheists and admirers of science fiction. The implications for such ideas as moral responsibility are mind-boggling.

To focus on your specific question: great scientists like Newton and Maxwell had no difficulty in combining a deep Christian faith with the idea that the fundamental equations of nature that they were elucidating were deterministic. But if the laws of physics were really fully deterministic, then it is hard to see how true free will could exist. Although many philosophers argue for a "compatabilist" view that free will and determinism can go together, this seems to us to be unpersuasive and motivated by a desire to evade the dilemma that physicalism denies free will. However, the "randomness" or, more precisely, the "uncertainty" that seems to be at the heart of the physical world does make it clearer how true freedom and free will could emerge. This is especially true if you combine the uncertainty at very small scales with the effects of chaotic dynamics, which can magnify the effects of extremely small changes as complex systems develop over time.

For example, there is now good evidence that the firing of an individual neuron can be influenced by the binding of just two calcium ions to receptors in that neuron, and although the mass of a neuron is almost certainly too high for quantum effects to be directly significant, the mass of a calcium ion certainly is not.

JP: Modern science has come to recognize that the processes that can give rise to genuine novelty have to be "at the edge of chaos" where order and disorder, chance and necessity, creatively interlace. Otherwise things are either too rigid for anything really new to happen or too haphazard for novelty to be able to persist. The intrinsic unpredictabilities of quantum mechanics and chaos theory can be seen theologically as gifts of a Creator whose creation is both orderly and open in this way.

20. What Is the Anthropic Principle?

Are you aware of the arguments of the anthropic principle? Do you think that Dawkins defeats them in The God Delusion*? What do* *you make of what he says, and what is exactly the force of the anthropic principle?*

NB & JP: We'll take this as two questions, dealing first with the fine-tuning argument and then with the attempted counterarguments offered by Dawkins.

Anthropic fine-tuning is a big topic that has been explored extensively, but the basic idea is easy to grasp. As far as we know at present there are six apparently fundamental constants in nature (see appendix A for details) whose values have to be very close to their presently observed values if any intelligent, carbon-based life is to come into being anywhere in the universe. In some cases these values have to be astonishingly accurate: for example, the parameter called lambda, which controls the long-range acceleration of the expansion of the universe in relativity, has to be a factor of 10^{120} smaller than such an explanation would have considered natural. Einstein actually thought that introducing lambda was his "greatest mistake" and that it should have been left out (which would have been equivalent to setting it to zero by definition), but careful measurements have shown that it is in fact slightly positive. It is now usually referred to as "dark energy."

As Tony Hewish once remarked, the accuracy of just one of these parameters is comparable to getting the mix of flour and sugar right to within one grain of sugar in a cake ten times the mass of the sun. Thus there are essentially only four possible explanations:

1. This fine-tuning is highly unlikely in a random possible universe, but God has ensured in his loving wisdom that it is so, so that we can come into being.
2. This fine-tuning is highly unlikely in a random possible universe, but just by luck the one that exists is anthropic.
3. This fine-tuning is highly unlikely in a random possible universe, but there are such a vast number of other universes that it is not unlikely that at least one of them is anthropic.

4. There are as yet undiscovered reasons why this fine-tuning is not highly unlikely in a random possible universe.

It's fair to say that pretty well all atheists with a scientific background who have seriously considered the matter are driven to explanation 3, explicitly to avoid number 1. And with very little other scientific motivation, possibility 2 is just too much of a cop-out. If the string/brane theorists are right and we are in a ten- or eleven-dimensional space-time and not a four-dimensional one, the chances are that there will be extra constants that are mysteriously fine-tuned, not fewer.

There is a lot of debate about the philosophical and meta-scientific significance of anthropic fine-tuning.[1] Clearly we can only raise the question because we are here, but such a remarkable number of coincidences surely demands to be made intelligible by some deeper explanation. Some cosmologists propose that it is the anthropic property that selects this universe to be actualized from the almost infinite number of other possible universes. But this is clearly not a scientific argument. As Stephen Hawking puts it in a recent paper, "A bottom-up approach to cosmology either requires one to postulate an initial state of the universe that is carefully fine-tuned—as if prescribed by an outside agency—or it requires one to invoke the notion of eternal inflation, a mighty speculative notion to the generation of many different universes, which prevents one from predicting what a typical observer would see."

Option 4 might correspond to the idea that the true fundamental theory (unifying relativity and quantum theory) has no arbitrary constant. This seems unlikely, and even if it were true, the fact that such abstract physical requirement led to anthropic fine-tuning is surely the most astonishing coincidence of all.

21. Have Anthropic Arguments Been Refuted?

NB & JP: Dawkins certainly doesn't defeat this argument in *The God Delusion*, although as we have repeatedly noted, the argument, while strongly suggestive, cannot be absolutely conclusive.

Like most biologists of his generation, Dawkins does not appear to be comfortable with detailed calculations. In his discussion of the anthropic principle he offers two attempted rebuttals:

1. It "can be answered by the suggestion . . . that there are many universes," and he goes on to discuss some variants of this idea.
2. "Any God capable of designing a universe, carefully and foresightfully tuned to lead to our evolution, must be a supremely complex and improbable entity who needs an even bigger explanation than the one he is supposed to provide."

We'll give simplified responses to these points here. Readers interested in details and nuances can consult appendix A.

Answering an argument by a suggestion is hardly conclusive, and the problem is that we don't just need a hundred other universes, or even one billion, but an utterly immense number—some string theorists suggest that there are up to 10^{500} other universes. If you are allowed to posit 10^{500} other universes to explain away otherwise inconvenient observations, you can "explain away" anything, and science becomes impossible.

Dawkins also advocates the "serial big crunch" model: the idea that the universe might expand and contract and then expand again with slightly different parameters, thus eventually having the right set of values. He is half-hearted about this idea and apparently doesn't realize that it is wholly nonviable. If any universe that is generated expands forever or fails to expand at all the series would terminate, and both these possibilities are quite likely.

Dawkins also likes Lee Smolin's idea of cosmological natural selection. It suggests that universes might be "born" mainly from black holes in other universes, that there might be small random variations in their fundamental constants, and that the fine-tuning of the parameters required for life might also sharply maximize the production of black holes. Given these assumptions, and a few others, the probability that a random universe in the hypothetical multiverse was anthropic would be quite high. Dawkins, alas, obscures the highly conjectural nature of these assumptions, each of which is implausible.

The first is doubly implausible because it requires not only that black holes act as "universe creation machines" but also that there are no other significant universe creation mechanisms, such as "eternal inflation," which has rather more theoretical backing—although there is certainly no firm evidence of either. The second is highly conjectural, which seems to violate one of the few "known" facts about black holes, which do not swallow up information as was first thought to be the case. On the third, Smolin makes a case that some of the possible variations in parameters would reduce the incidence of black holes—not nearly enough is known about all the processes involved to be certain. But it is not enough for this idea to work that the number of black holes is maximized in the anthropic case. It has to be maximized so sharply that the probability of an anthropic universe is high. A simple example will illustrate the point. If I toss a fair coin four times and get exactly two heads, it is not surprising: not only is it the most likely outcome but the probability is 37.5 percent. However, if I toss it a thousand times and get exactly five hundred heads, although this is still the "most probable" single outcome, the probability is only 2.5 percent. With one million tosses the probability of getting exactly 500,000 heads is minute. Furthermore, unless it turns out to be logically necessary that the universe/multiverse has the properties that Smolin needs (which is wildly implausible), we would still be left with the remarkable anthropic coincidence that the universe happened to have just those properties that enabled "cosmic natural selection" to produce anthropic universes.

Let's now deal with Dawkins's second objection, the claim that God must be complex and hence "improbable." There are many confusions here, and it is hard to know where to begin.

The whole question of complexity and simplicity is more subtle than he seems to realize. Consider for example a right-angled triangle two sides of which have length 1. The length of the third side is, of course, $\sqrt{2}$, which is a highly "improbable" number that in decimal form consists of an infinite, nonrepeating sequence of digits. But it is simple to specify. Furthermore, if the triangle in question is made of some suitably exotic material (perhaps some nanomaterial carefully arranged to be a catalyst), then the actual nature of the third side of this triangle could be very difficult to specify precisely. Nevertheless you can make precise and simple statements about its length, using the simple concept of $\sqrt{2}$, and indeed from this you could make specific and useful predictions, such as the rate at which this catalyst would work.

In fact, in much of science we use theories that are fairly simple to specify but have complex implications. You can write down the Einstein equation (for general relativity) on a postage stamp (see appendix A). However, the implications of this equation and its solutions are of mind-boggling complexity: in most cases no exact solutions can be found, but the behavior of pretty much all the matter in the universe (neglecting quantum effects) can be "explained" by this equation. By Dawkins's "argument" we should reject the Einstein equation, and its cousin the Dirac equation (equally simple to write down and one that "explains" the behavior of pretty much all matter in the universe neglecting the effect of general relativity), because anything that offers such an explanation must be supremely complex and improbable. We agree, of course, that it is remarkable that such simple and beautiful equations seem to describe so much about the universe—one that is explained by the existence of a loving ultimate Creator and left wholly unexplained by Dawkins and his atheist colleagues.

Now, the comparable assertion to the Einstein equation that Christians make is as follows: There exists a loving ultimate Creator who has revealed himself in Jesus of Nazareth. The comparable assertion for Judaism might be "There exists a loving ultimate Creator revealed in the (Hebrew) Bible." It is perfectly clear that we have here a simple specification even though the implications are astonishingly complex and wonderful.

At this point Dawkins or his defenders may object that he is not saying that the assertion of the existence of God is complex but that God is complex. However, both the Einstein and Dirac equations implicitly assert the existence of highly "complex" entities (such as the space-time manifold and the quantum vacuum), but the point is that they can be specified simply. If Dawkins's "argument" against the existence of God were valid, then it would also be a valid argument against all of fundamental physics.

There are a couple of further points that apply specifically to God. The first is the doctrine of divine simplicity. Dawkins has heard of this doctrine. Having attributed, however, the bizarre view to Richard Swinburne that "God constantly keeps a finger on each and every particle," he goes on to assert that "[a] God capable of continuously monitoring and controlling the individual status of every particle in the universe cannot be simple." But he gives no justification for this view, which seems to rest on the assumption that God gets his knowledge and exercises his powers in the same way that we do, via brains, computers, instruments, or other complex physical entities. No serious theist suggests this idea—and, as Swinburne says, whether a hypothesis is simple or not is an intrinsic feature of that hypothesis, not a matter of its relation to observable data.

Let me take another analogy from physics. It is thought that the Higgs field in some sense gives mass to all the particles in the universe. If this were a theological entity, Dawkins might describe it as "keeping a finger on each and every particle" and conclude that the Higgs field is "too complex." It is an exciting and currently open question whether or not the Higgs field actually exists—most physicists think it does, and the hope is that the new facility at CERN called LHC will settle the question. But no serious scientist or philosopher is deterred from believing in the Higgs field by considerations such as those advanced by Dawkins.

The second is a rather simpler point: Christians assert the existence of an ultimate Creator. To ask, "Who created the ultimate Creator" or "What explains the ultimate Creator" is simply to show that you have not understood the meaning of the term. From a philosophical point of view, an ultimate Creator might or might not exist, but unless you can show that the concept of an ultimate Creator is genuinely logically impossible—and even Dawkins doesn't think that this is the case—you cannot meaningfully ask for an explanation of the ultimate Creator's existence.

JP: Part of the theological meaning of divine simplicity is that in God essence and existence coincide, so that the deity is a self-sustaining being with no need for reliance on any other source of origin.

22. Why Is the Universe So Big?

Does the sheer vastness of the universe make the inference to God based on fine-tuning less compelling? Couldn't one argue that God wasted a lot of space (no pun intended) in order to create life?

NB & JP: The size of the universe is essentially a function of its age. We need enough time to create second-generation stars, and then for life to evolve, so 13.7 billion years seem about right. If all the 10^{22} stars of the observable universe were not there, we would not be here to be daunted by cosmic immensity. In many respects there is no real difference between 14 thousand years, 14 million years, and 14 billion years: they are all immense to us, and all equally comprehensible to God.

The fine-tuning is, of course, about the fundamental constants of nature, which (as far as we know) are the same throughout the universe.

23. Will Everything, Eventually, Be Explained by Science?

When you talk about systems, you seem surprised at patterns that appear seemingly magically out of your perceived probability of randomness. I dispute that this is remarkable. It is only systems that are not well understood (yet) that seem to produce magical results. The fact that we are all here, the things you describe, the air you are breathing . . . they exist. That is all. It cannot be explained. Everything else, all arguments pointing to something mysterious, something not yet discovered, something science has overlooked or cannot explain may well be explained one day.

NB & JP: The fact that we and anything else exists is indeed remarkable in itself, but in addition it turns out that if the known laws of physics or their constants were even slightly different, no form of life could exist anywhere in the universe, a discovery that was quite unexpected and also remarkable. Furthermore, the ways in which deep order arises apparently spontaneously from chaotic systems is also very surprising—it is becoming understood a bit better and John's idea that "active information" is a causal principle seems to have increasing merit.

We don't suggest that the emergence of new and remarkable complexity in a system "on the edge of chaos" is miraculous or magical—it turns out to be a consequence of the deep mathematical structure of the laws of nature. But what the emergence of complexity does do is to allow new causal principles to come into play. With even a slight indeterminacy, the behavior of such systems is no longer completely determined by the "low-level" laws and adds a logic of its own.

Something like this seems to happen with the emergence of life and of consciousness. In fact, the distinguished evolutionist Simon Conway Morris suggests that evolution, far from being blindly random in the way that is often suggested, is "Darwin's search engine." The repeated independent emergence in the course of evolution of basic structures, such as the eyes, suggests that there is a deep-seated bias towards fruitful development present in the structure of nature. The theist will see this as a sign of divinely purposed fertility.

24. Is a Unified Theory of Everything Possible?

Do you agree with Stanley Jaki's invocation of Gödel's incompleteness theorem as an argument against the possibility of developing a theory of everything that is "necessarily," not just "contingently," true? Hawking, as I understand it, even admits that Gödel's work will complicate the consistency of a unified theory, does he not? If Gödel's work does throw a wrench into the works, why hasn't the physics community caught on to this? Why, after his many walks with Gödel in Princeton, was Einstein not dissuaded from pursuing a grand unified theory?

NB: A grand unified theory isn't really a "theory of everything" in the sense of predicting everything. Gödel certainly shows that there are limits to mathematical and scientific knowledge even within the domains in which you would expect them to apply. But no wise philosopher claims that science can fully explain everything.

Gödel's incompleteness theorem is so counterintuitive to people who have been trained in the classical logical tradition that it is not surprising that even such a great genius as Einstein didn't fully see the implications. Also, Gödel was eccentric to the point of madness, and this may possibly have made Einstein reluctant to think that Gödel had said the last word on the subject. However, Einstein was also very aware that his endeavors might not be successful.

It is certainly striking that modern science arose in Christian societies in Western Europe and not in the much richer societies of India and China or in the intellectually lively ambient of ancient Greece. Many scholars argue that this was no accident, and that belief in a loving ultimate Creator, whose free choice of cosmic order could only be discovered by investigating the actual nature of creation, played a significant role.

JP: Gödel's theorem shows us that truth can never be totally caught in any purely logical system—a useful lesson I think. It seems that truth always exceeds what can be proved by logic. This fact certainly provides a significant check to grandiose claims about theories of everything. Stanley Jaki is very learned and interesting to read. I think that Christian belief in creation was an influence on the birth of modern science in twelfth-century Europe, but I would not go so far as Jaki's claim that this belief, then and now, is indispensible to a fruitful science.

Further Studies

Barrow, J. D., and F. J. Tipler. 1986. *The Anthropic Cosmological Principle*. Oxford: Oxford University Press.

Carr, Bernard, ed. 2007 *Universe or Multiverse?* Cambridge: Cambridge University Press.

Gumbel, Nicky. 2008. *Is God a Delusion?* London: Alpha International.

Holder, Rodney. 2004. *God, The Multiverse, and Everything: Modern Cosmology and the Argument from Design*. Aldershot: Ashgate.

Polkinghorne, John. 2006. *Science and Creation: The Search for Understanding*. Philadelphia: Templeton Foundation Press.

Russell, R. J., N. Murphy, and C. J. Isham, eds. 1996. *Quantum Cosmology and the Laws of Nature: Scientific Perspectives on Divine Action.* 2d ed. Vatican City: Vatican Observatory.

Swinburne, Richard. 2004. *The Existence of God.* 2d ed. Oxford: Oxford University Press.

Ward, Keith. 2008. *Why There Almost Certainly Is a God.* Oxford: Lion.

4
Evolution

In responses here, we present a condensed version of a longer and more technical discussion given in appendix C.

25. Is Evolution Fact or Theory?

NB & JP: The Bible affirms that in the beginning God *created* the heavens and the earth (or as we would now put it, the entire universe) and that through his creative Word, order, life and humanity eventually came into being. It is not concerned with the scientific details of the process as is clearly shown by the fact that there are two creation accounts in Genesis that differ in detail. And one aspect of his creating human beings "in his own image" is that we are given minds able to understand, at least in part, some of the scientific principles involved.

Newton made a huge breakthrough when he showed how you could account for the motion of the planets and many other material objects through a simple law of gravitation. Newton was a devout, though somewhat unorthodox, Christian. And although some atheist philosophers tried to infer from this a mechanistic and atheistic worldview, no one now seriously suggests that gravity undermines the Bible—indeed we see it as a wonderful insight into the faithful regularity of God that the universe is ruled by laws that we are able to discern.

Darwin and Mendel laid the foundations of a comparable breakthrough when they realized, respectively, that natural selection and what we now call genetics could account for the origin of the species. At one level, evolution is a purely mathematical observation: given a population of any kind (animals, viruses, languages, or objects in a computer simulation) where there is replication, mutation, and selection then the equations of evolutionary dynamics will apply and will give insights, often very profound, into what is going on. However, by "evolution" we mean the remarkable scientific discovery that all known species appear to be related to each other in ways that can be described and analyzed by evolutionary processes. The genetic evidence for this is now completely overwhelming (see appendix C). In this respect, evolution is like gravity. Gravity influences everything in the universe—but it is not the *whole* story of matter. Similarly, evolution influences everything in the biosphere, but it is not the whole story. And it is now clear that genetic evolution is not the whole story of evolution, with epigenetic and cultural factors also being important.

Evolution does not contradict the Bible, which says that "God formed man from the dust of the earth," any more than astrophysics contradicts the Bible when it says that God also made the stars. Evolution and astrophysics give an insight into the scientific details of *how* God did these things, which are not what the Bible is about. The Bible gives insights into the much more important ethical and spiritual realities—remember that people used to *worship* stars and planets, and, in some cases, make human sacrifices to them.

A belief in evolution does not imply atheism. Darwin was at pains to make this point, and many of the greatest scientists who developed the modern understanding of evolution, such as Mendel, Fisher, and Dobzhansky, were Christians, as are leading contemporary evolutionists like Simon Conway Morris and Martin Nowak. The idea that the religious establishment opposed Darwin is a complete fabrication.

Just as the deep insights of Newton laid the foundations for the even deeper insights of Faraday, Maxwell, Einstein, and their successors, there is little doubt that the more we develop a detailed quantitative understanding of evolutionary dynamics, systems biology, and so forth, the more we will discover unexpected new processes and phenomena. There may be natural tendencies in matter to spontaneously generate certain types of complex structure that are biologically accessible and functionally effective (see, e.g., Stuart Kauffman, *At Home in the Universe*). The history of life seems to have converged many times on certain types of solutions (Simon Conway Morris, *Life's Solution*). The religious believer will see these factors as signs of the inherent potentiality with which the Creator has endowed creation.

Evolutionary processes are widespread in cosmic history. The coming to be of stars and galaxies can be seen, in a generalized sense, as an evolutionary process. At the heart of evolution is the interplay between "chance" (the contingent detail of what actually happens) and "necessity" (the lawfully regular environment in which events occur). It takes place "at the edge of chaos," where order and openness interlace. If things are too orderly, they are too rigid for anything really new to emerge. If they are too haphazard, nothing that emerged could persist. From a theological point of view, we can see necessity as the gift of that reliability to creation that reflects the Creator's steadfast faithfulness, and chance as the loving gift of a free openness within which creatures can explore God-given potentiality in a process by which they are allowed to "make themselves." Such a world is surely a greater good than a ready-made world would have been.

26. What about Intelligent Design?

NB & JP: The U.S. Constitution prohibits Congress from making laws respecting an establishment of religion or prohibiting the free exercise thereof. This is interpreted as imposing a pretty strict separation of church and state. So practices with religious overtones in schools that would be quite normal in the UK—and were so in the U.S. in the recent past—have been declared unconstitutional by U.S. courts. Combining this with the fundamental misconception that evolution is incompatible with Christianity and the misuse of the word "creationist" to mean "someone who believes in creation as opposed to evolution" rather than "someone who believes in creation" has led to a situation in the United States that is fraught with confusion.

Of course God is "intelligent," and of course teaching in schools that "godless evolution" is the only story is intellectually and spiritually impoverishing. But evolution is no more "godless" than gravity or electromagnetism.

God is never spoken of as a "designer" in the Bible: he is Creator and Father, and a Father does not "design" his children. Even a great creative writer does not exactly "design" her or his characters, and in any performance, whether of a play or a piece of music, the individual decisions and actions of the performers are vital elements in addition to the intentions of the playwright or composer. By endowing us with free will and giving us the capacity to love, God calls us to be in a limited but very important sense co-creators. To the extent that the U.S. legal position forces people to use the language of design, it is understandable that they do so, but nevertheless unfortunate.

The proponents of intelligent design also make a scientific claim of identifying molecular biological systems of "irreducible complexity," but we do not believe they have made their case or are ever likely to do so. It is not enough to consider a single system in isolation, since evolution works in an improvisatory way, co-opting what has been useful for one purpose to help achieve another. Furthermore, even if one biochemical mechanism could be found where the probability of its evolving was extremely low, since evolution is inherently probabilistic, it would not be convincing evidence that evolution was wrong.

Intelligent design advocates also seem tacitly to make the theological mistake of assuming that God, who is the creator and sustainer of nature, would not be content to work through natural processes, which in fact are as much expressions of the divine will as choosing to work directly.

27. Can the Mind Be Explained by Evolution?

I viewed a recent discussion on the topic of whether our thoughts are material. The Christian holds that the process of thought is material but thought itself is not. Atheists generally hold that all processes and outcomes of thought are solely material. They claim that all neuroscientists would agree. What are the implications for the Christian if our thoughts are wholly material?

NB: This is a complex topic that we address in some detail in appendix B. Let's try and give an outline of our position here.

First, even computer software isn't "material" in any normal sense. Consider a piece of software like Firefox, the open-source Web browser. Where is it? It is installed in millions of computers worldwide. It is downloaded thousands of times a day. While it is being downloaded each copy may pass through twenty or more computers. Master copies of the software are stored on a number of different servers, and within each server they may be striped across several physical disks, so that no single material failure can destroy the software. These disks will be backed up repeatedly. We're not, of course, suggesting that there is anything supernatural about computer software; we're merely pointing out that it is not "material" in any normal sense of the word. The only coherent language to use is to say that it has representations in or on material objects, but it is not to be identified with any particular set of representations.

Now consider something like *Hamlet* or J. S. Bach's Mass in B Minor. No manuscript of *Hamlet* survives, and there are three distinct printed sources that differ in detail. Almost every performance uses a slightly different text: there are at least fourteen different editions, and performances are generally cut. It is absurd to identify any individual material object with the play itself. Furthermore, even if all the paper copies of Hamlet were destroyed, there are still innumerable copies on CDs, DVDs, and tapes and in cyberspace. There is an original manuscript of the Mass in B Minor, but there are emendations thought to be by Bach's son. Therefore, there are significant differences in the various printed editions. Each performance of the Mass in B Minor is different, and there are hundreds of recordings and millions of copies of these. Again, it makes sense to say that various material objects are representations of the Mass in B Minor, but we deny that the Mass in B Minor is itself a material object. It transcends its particular representations.

If we grant the point that works of music, art, and literature can exist without being "material" objects, it is logical that works of music, art, and literature can be seen as instances of ideas. And it makes much more sense to consider thoughts to be ideas rather than material objects. Thoughts have many of the properties of music and literature that we discussed, and considering thoughts as ideas allows for the possibility of two persons having the same thought in different places, which is tricky for a material object. Furthermore, because brains are hypercomplex systems and truly subject to chaotic dynamics and quantum effects, they are not fully predictable at a physical level and thus ripe for being subject to causation from "active information." Since our knowledge of matter and physics comes from our minds and thoughts, one would need overwhelming evidence to show that minds and thoughts don't really exist but that physical objects and matter do.

This is not to say that all forms of physicalism are contradictory—such a strong result, alas, never occurs in philosophy. But physicalists have to deny the real existence of many more entities that are generally taken as existing than thoughts, and the only remotely compelling reason that might be offered for accepting physicalism—namely, that "science has shown that all our thoughts are determined by physical laws"—can now, for reasons we discuss in appendix B, be seen to be incorrect.

JP: Of course, thinking is an activity that has a material substrate, but I believe that the relationship of mind and brain is best understood in terms of the view of dual-aspect monism, linking the material and the mental to form a complementary relationship, rather than through a fallacious attempt to reduce the mental to the material.

28. Isn't Evolution Unethical?

Should Christians simply accept evolution as science but refrain from becoming social Darwinists? Can a Christian who accepts evolution still take Christian living as seriously as the early church did? Does it put restraints on traditional Christian ethics, such as caring for the poor, sick, etc.?

NB & JP: Spencer's "survival of the fittest" and other attempts to make a secular religion out of evolution should be resisted. Darwin himself was dead against them as well. It is only the *scientific* aspects of evolutionary theory that should be embraced. Remember, people in the eighteenth century tried to do the same with Newtonian mechanics—and no one now thinks that gravity is incompatible with Christianity.

True altruism exceeds kin altruism (within the family gene pool) or reciprocal altruism (helping another in the expectation of return). When someone risks his or her life in order to save an unknown and unrelated child from a burning building, there is altruism of an order that exceeds evolutionary explanation. Darwinian thinking on its own is ethically inadequate, as Richard Dawkins acknowledges on the last page of *The Selfish Gene*. After 214 pages claiming that human beings are merely genetic survival machines, on the last page he says, "We, alone on earth, can rebel against the tyranny of the selfish replicators." Dawkins obviously (and rightly) thinks we should, but he has not learned that lesson from evolutionary biology. Although a great deal is now understood about the conditions under which "altruistic" behavior will evolve in populations, this is neither a substitute for ethics, nor does it explain ethics away. It is interesting, for example, that the evolutionary dynamics of the superiority of forgiveness over revenge or even tit-for-tat is now quite well understood. But this doesn't address the ethical or spiritual aspects at all, merely the practical consequences, which, although relevant, are not decisive. After all, "take up your cross" is hardly an invitation to worldly success.

29. Why Is Evolution So Wasteful?

Does the apparent wastefulness of natural selection go some way to discrediting the idea that God is loving and merciful? How can a God of love allow a creation to develop where so many species die in (often) horrific and protracted suffering? I appreciate the idea that life was given the freedom to "make itself," but still the developmental process that leads to sentiency seems nonsensically brutal.

NB & JP: Well, "species" don't suffer. Clearly some higher animals do, although we must avoid the "pathetic fallacy" of attributing human feeling to nonhumans.

The problem of pain—even when we eliminate the doubtful cases—is a real and serious one. But no one has ever suggested a better way than natural selection to allow life to "make itself." In fact, some suggest that it is the only possible way.

The questioner queries whether the good of human creators' making themselves outweighs the scale of suffering and wastefulness apparently involved. The issue is a serious one, though its answering is beyond the power of human calculation. If that self-making involves the bringing to birth of potentiality through the shuffling explorations of contingent chance, the process will inevitably involve not only great fruitfulness but also ragged edges and blind alleys.

Further Studies

Alexander, Denis. 2008. *Creation and Evolution: Do We Have to Choose?* Oxford: Monarch.

Desmond, Adrian, and John Moore. 1991. *Darwin.* London: Michael Joseph.

McGrath, Alister E. 2009. *A Fine-Tuned Universe: The Quest for God in Science and Theology.* Louisville, KY: Westminster John Knox Press.

Noble, Denis, 2006. *The Music of Life*. Oxford: Oxford University Press.

Peacocke, Arthur. 2004. *Creation and the World of Science*. Rev. ed. Oxford: Oxford University Press.

Ruse, Michael. 2000. *Can a Darwinian Be a Christian? The Relationship between Science and Religion*. Cambridge: Cambridge University Press.

5
Evil

30. Where Does Evil Come From?

If God is good, how can God put a world into being that is not perfectly good? I used to think that evil was the result of free will, but if evolution is true, then there was evil before free will. Believing that all evil will eventually disappear forever does not, however, in my opinion, absolve God from allowing evil into this world in the first place. As I look at it now, evil in a Darwinist world suggests a dualistic God, who created both good and evil, and is hence both good and evil. That would not leave much room for the Christian God. I hope you can shed some light on this.

NB: The problem of evil is a serious one, and I'm not sure that it makes much difference whether one is "creationist" or not. We cannot "solve" it in this simple note, but perhaps a few thoughts help:

We know God loves us, and we know there is evil in the world. God must have good enough reasons for allowing the evil to exist. But it is absurd to suggest that we should necessarily know what God's reasons are. In the book of Job, God is not simply saying, "I'm bigger than you are," which would be a vacuous *non*-response, but rather, "You cannot expect to understand my purposes." Alvin Plantinga has the metaphor of comparing the statements "There is an elephant in my tent" and "There is a particularly small but nastily biting insect in my tent." If you reply "But I cannot see the elephant," then, under normal conditions, this would be a good reason to believe that an elephant was not, in fact, in the tent (philosophers call this a "defeater"). But it is not a good defeater to reply, "I cannot see the insect." So the following suggestions by no means exhaust all the possibilities.

Much of the evil that exists is directly or indirectly the result of human sin—that is, falling short of the glory of God. In addition to the obvious ways in which this is true (murder, etc.), biological death was apparently in the world long before Adam and Eve, but the sting of death was perhaps intensified by the emergence of morally conscious beings: someone in perfect loving union with God might not feel the pain of separation brought by death nearly as much as we do. This is not to deny the terrible reality of death, but to affirm that it is not final.

The evil that is not the result of human sin seems to be the result of the workings out of the natural laws of physics (e.g., earthquakes) and biology (e.g., viruses). It may well be necessary to have such laws in order that beings can emerge who are free to choose to love. And surely a universe without pain but also lacking in freely given love would be worse than one with both. The new creation at the "end of time" is possible only and precisely because the people in it have lived through the present creation and have freely chosen the path of love.

We know that God doesn't merely allow suffering while being a passive spectator, but suffered himself on the cross. He carries our sorrows and redeems them. While it is true that "the sufferings of this present time are not worthy to be compared with the glory which shall be revealed" (Rom. 8:18 KJV) it is not the whole story. There must be a sense in which these sufferings are necessary, and perhaps the previous discussion gives some hints about this. But "now we see through a glass, darkly" (1 Cor. 13:12 KJV).

JP: My thinking on the perplexing problem of evil is very much along the lines of Nicholas's reply. Natural evil is the inescapable shadow side of an evolving fruitful world (see question 14).

As we noted earlier, the existence of tectonic plates allows mineral resources to well up in the gaps between them, thereby replenishing the surface of the earth, but it also allows earthquakes and tsunamis to occur. You cannot have the one without the other.

31. Who or What Is "the Devil"?

While I realize many thoughtful Christians (like C. S. Lewis) believed in demons and the devil, and it's in Scripture, the concept has become difficult for me to swallow. The "red guy with a pitchfork" is a poor conceptualization, and so is the idea that all human actions of "evil' on this planet are somehow the end-products of his or his invisible minions' temptations.

NB: It's very hard to know what to think about Satan, demons, and angels. The Bible says little about them. Angels seem to be spiritual beings who worship God but are occasionally sent to be his messengers on earth. The biblical picture of Satan (which means "the accuser" in Hebrew) seems to vary: in the prologue to Job (Job, by the way, is, roughly, a play and not intended to be historical, but it is one of the most profound books in the Bible) he's a kind of rogue courtier, but Jesus talks about him as the fundamental quasi-personal influence behind much of the evil in the world.

When Jesus says to Peter, "'Get behind me, Satan! You do not have in mind the things of God, but the things of men'" (Mark 8:33 and par. NIV), he is not suggesting that Peter is "possessed" by the devil or that Peter is not making these very prudent suggestions for his Master's safety of his own free will. He seems to be saying that Peter is unwittingly falling in with Satan's designs. Thus, describing Satan as the ultimate "force" behind the sin in the world does not mean that humans are absolved of their responsibilities. But the Bible is clear that there is a cosmic struggle going on and not just a human one.

It's tempting to use the language of chaos theory here and make the analogy between Satan and a "strange attractor," which is a dynamical path (of non-integer dimension) that is not necessarily reached by other dynamical paths in the system, but whose existence and characteristics influence the behaviors of the dynamical paths that come near it.

JP: All I would add to Nicholas's helpful response is that when one considers a terrible event like the Holocaust, there are of course human factors at work (the wills of wicked men, the social sin of unquestioning obedience to the state, ordinary people's compromises and cowardice), but the weight of evil involved is so great that I myself cannot rule out the influence of some form of evil spiritual power at work. Where such a power came from and why it is allowed to operate are, of course, very perplexing questions.

I do not quite know what to think about angels. One problem is that both in Hebrew (Old Testament) and in Greek (New Testament) the word thus translated is the perfectly ordinary word for a messenger. Some of these messengers may simply have been human beings. At other times, it is possible that contemporary culture encouraged using the figure of an angel symbolically to represent the reception of a divinely inspired message (just as demon possession could be used figuratively for what we would in our culture recognize as disease).

32. Why Is There Cancer?

You said in your St. Edmund's Lecture (2002), "The same cellular processes that have driven the fruitful history of evolution through genetic mutation must necessarily allow other cells to mutate and become malignant. The anguishing fact that there is cancer in creation is not gratuitous, something that a more compassionate or competent Creator could easily have remedied."

Could God not have guided evolution so that we have bodies which attempt to kill off cells that mutate and become malignant?

NB: Well, he has/we do—there is a wonderful and elaborate immune system whose mysteries we are only just beginning to fathom, but the immune system is not infallible, and we develop cancer and other diseases when the immune response is insufficient to prevent the disease. I think the fundamental reason the immune system is not infallible is that it is built with stochastic processes and also that if the immune responses are too strong then (a) you get autoimmune diseases and (b) the energy used is excessive. John's fundamental point—that it is the same molecular processes—of course remains.

JP: See the responses to questions 5, 9, and 14.

33. Is Original Sin a Result of Nature or Nurture?

Is original sin genetic or largely societal? Hasn't every individual person become corrupted through his or her own choices? I agree with you that we're responsible for our own sins, not those of Adam and Eve. But sin entered the world through their sins, and everyone after them has become corrupted by it through their own free choice. Am I right on this?

NB: Adam is the first true man, not biologically (the Bible clearly implies there were others of the same species) but spiritually—that is, capable of being in communion with God and rejecting his commands. As for the idea that the first spiritually aware human beings were also the first to disobey God's commands, this is sadly all too probable.

It seems clear to me that in a sense the first time *we* sin we become corrupted by our own sin—not by the sin of any of our ancestors. However, in a certain sense it is all one sin, and at a psychological level, it is much easier to sin if other people are doing it.

I don't think pre-fall humans are in a higher state than we are, for Jesus has done more than restore us to a pre-fall condition: he has made it possible for us to become adopted children of God. However, pre-fall humans are in a higher state than unredeemed humans—so is a little child, as Jesus seems to indicate.

If God had made us in such a way that we were incapable of sin, he would have made us without free will, but then we would have been incapable of love. He creates, amazingly, a universe in which we are free to choose to love—that inevitably means that we are free to choose to sin. He deals with the sin, on the cross, and the potential for love is infinite.

JP: It is interesting that the powerful story of Genesis 3 depicts the fall as a fall upwards: the gaining of the knowledge of good and evil! At some point in hominid evolution, self-consciousness—a deep self-awareness and the power to project our thought far into the future—dawned on our ancestors. At the same time, I believe that a new form of God-consciousness also dawned for them. The fall was the process by which they turned away from God into the self, an error of which we are all the heirs. This did not bring biological death into the world, since that had been there for many millions of years, but it brought what one might call mortality, human sadness at the transience of life. Because our ancestors were self-conscious, they knew that eventually they would die. Because they had alienated themselves from the One whose faithfulness is the sole (and sufficient) ground of the hope of destiny beyond death, this knowledge became a source of deep sadness.

34. Why Do People Choose Evil?

It seems that our free will chooses that which is in accordance with our nature. If God gave to man a nature that delighted in the good, that is, one in accordance with God's will, then man would choose with his free will to do that which was pleasing to his nature and therefore pleasing to God. But humans seem not to have been given such a nature. It seems that God then judges humans for the failure of the defective nature that he gave them. Is there any problem with my suggestion?

NB: The point about free will is that it is free. Although the impulse to do good is (in fact) very strong in humanity, God has given us a nature in which it is not always overwhelming because otherwise we would not be free.

However, although our free choices to act in ways that separate us from God (i.e., our sins) do indeed lead to judgment (because God is just), he has, at infinite cost, made it possible for every one of us to be redeemed from these failures to love through the perfect love of his son. So the incarnation is the remedy for our fallenness—which is what the church fathers meant by saying that Christ is the "second Adam."

JP: Philosophers have debated whether it is a consistent possibility that beings could be created who always freely agree to do good. Nicholas and I agree with the majority that this is not a coherent possibility. (See John Hick, *Evil and the God of Love*, 113–19.)

35. Does Religion Inspire Evil Acts?

NB & JP: Any religious person has to acknowledge with regret and penitence that evil acts have been done in the name of religion. The sad history of crusades and inquisitions makes the point. One must also recognize the many good and fruitful acts of care and compassion that religion has inspired, as well as much creativity in music and the arts.

The record of nonreligious people is certainly no better—we've already mentioned Hitler, Stalin, and Pol Pot in the twentieth century. The truth of the matter is that evil acts arise neither from religion nor lack of religion, as such, but from an inherent flaw in human nature that often turns a country's liberator into its next tyrant. Christianity calls this human slantedness "sin" and diagnoses its origin as a refusal to acknowledge that we are creatures who need the grace and guidance that, in fact, our Creator offers to us. "Doing it my way" is so often the recipe for moral disaster.

It is a wise saying that "the corruption of the best is the worst." When religion goes wrong, it can do so in very destructive ways, but this is a distortion of its true inspiration.

Further Studies

Hick, John. 1978. *Evil and the God of Love*. Rev. ed. San Francisco: Harper San Francisco.

Plantinga, Alvin. 1977. *God, Freedom, and Evil*. Grand Rapids: Eerdmans.

Polkinghorne, John. 2005. *Exploring Reality: The Intertwining of Science and Religion*. London: SPCK.

van Inwagen, Peter. 2004. *Christian Faith and the Problem of Evil*. Grand Rapids: Eerdmans.

6
Human Being

36. Who Were Adam and Eve?

Do you agree that Adam and Eve are the first actual human beings (or symbols of a group of the first ones as John interprets it) who possessed all the cognitive and moral/spiritual faculties necessary for knowing God, who evolved as you say 100,000 or so years ago and lived in harmony with God in the beatific garden of Eden for an unknown amount of time and, through their own free will, rejected God for the idolization of the self, resulting in the catastrophic fall?

NB: If we accept that there are now spiritually conscious human beings, and that there was a time in the past when there were none, then there must have been a time when this property first emerged in humanity. The word *adam* in Hebrew means "man" and is not really a proper name: by Adam and Eve we mean the first morally and spiritually conscious human beings. It is therefore somewhat curious when people doubt their existence. As I suggested in the last chapter, Adam is the first true man, not biologically but spiritually (i.e., capable of being in communion with God and rejecting his commands), and it is sadly all too probable that the first spiritually conscious human beings were also the first to disobey God's commands.

37. What Does It Mean to Be Created "in the Image of God"?

Genesis 1:26–27 says that humans are created in the image of God. What does this mean?

NB: First of all, nothing we can say can exhaust the richness of Scripture. The language of Genesis was inspired and speaks of things that are "too deep for words" (Rom. 8:26). Being made in God's image clearly does not mean we are like God in every respect, but that in very important respects we are an *ikon* of God. I think the main threads are as follows:

1. We are persons, capable of true love—and hence endowed with free will and living in a universe with "free processes"—reasonably but not totally predictable.
2. We are capable of moral choices.
3. We are intrinsically part of a loving community. The fact that the Trinity was present at creation adds an extra dimension to "let *us* make . . . *male and female* created He them."
4. We are intrinsically valuable in God's eyes.
5. We are creative—indeed called to be co-creators.
6. We are capable, by God's grace and redemption, of perfect union with God—Jesus is "the (perfect) image of the invisible God."

JP: Just a few more thoughts one might add:

Debate about the meaning of the "image of God" has gone on for centuries in the Christian community. Nicholas is right that it is a very rich and multifaceted concept. Other components include the following:

7. Science's power to fathom the deep structure of the universe, which I believe to be a pale reflection of our being in the Creator's image.

8. The granting of "dominion," understood in the sense of a caring shepherd-king rather than an exploitative despot, and perhaps also linked with the custom in the ancient world for absent kings to erect statuary images of themselves to recall their authority exercised through local vice-regents.

I think one of the most important meanings is point 4 (valuable in God's eyes), which liberates us from taking too functional a view of God's gift (rationality, etc.). The fundamental worth of the gravely handicapped surely derives from the fact that they too are bearers of the divine image.

38. When Does an Embryo Become a Person?

I heard Dr. Polkinghorne speak today . . . after the lecture he allowed a few questions. One had to do with the morality of embryonic stem cell research. Dr. Polkinghorne answered by discussing at what point an embryo becomes a human person (at fourteen days, I think). I would like to ask how the love principle—that God created a universe that allows beings to be and make themselves—would address this issue. If the potential for human life exists in the embryo before fourteen days, should love allow it to become?

NB: The issues here are quite complex. There is no doubt that human life begins at conception and that the other stages of life's way, although significant, are in some sense rather arbitrary milestones. Equally, a very large number of embryos will never, in the natural course of events, become human beings—often because of some genetic defect. Neither we nor the church has ever mourned the death of an early embryo in the way that one would mourn the loss of a human being. But many Christians (I think in particular of one Catholic doctor and scientist whose views I respect deeply) take the view that any potentially viable embryo should have the moral status of an infant, and that although we don't know which ones are viable and which are not, God does. Aquinas thought, following the science of his day, that the embryo/fetus goes through three stages of "ensoulment": first as a living thing, then as an animal, and finally as a human being. He is comparing and contrasting "the mode and order of Christ's conception" with that of other men, and he follows (and endorses) the prevailing scientific understanding due to Aristotle that the embryo goes through three stages: is first of all a living thing, and afterwards, an animal, and after that, a human. Although he was of course wrong about the biological details, if it is true that the soul is related to the active information embodied in the human body, then it is logical to see some such development. Part of the motivation for the idea that embryos after fourteen days have a special status is that this corresponds to the earliest development of the "primitive streak," and thus before then they do not have a nervous system of any kind.

JP: The embryo is human life from the start, and deserves high moral respect because of that, but I do not think that initially it has the absolute ethical status of personhood. This is something that I believe we grow into with increasing complexity of being. I personally am happy with the "fourteen-day rule" incorporated into UK legislation, which requires embryo research to take place only in that very early period. A large percentage (somewhere between 60 percent and 75 percent) of embryos conceived are believed not to implant. If all these were truly human persons, it would seem to imply that heaven will be largely populated by those who have never lived an independent life.

39. Do We Have Souls?

I have read about Stuart Hameroff and Roger Penrose's theory of quantum consciousness. They have constructed a theory according to which human consciousness is the result of quantum gravity effects in microtubules, which they dubbed Orch-OR. Others, including Max Tegmark, have been critical of this theory. I would very much like to know what you think of this theory and the crit-

icism it has received. Does this theory support the claim that the human soul is something separate from our physical bodies?

NB: The view that John and I share is that the soul is something *logically* distinct from our physical bodies, but not a separable physical entity. To give an analogy: imagine beautiful music being improvised on a piano. The piano is an essential requirement for the music, but the music is logically distinct from the piano: it could in principle be played on another piano—but it is not something completely separate from any instrument.

One of the attractions of Hameroff and Penrose's ideas is that they offer some kind of a framework within which we can think about our minds as not being completely deterministic. If the brain were simply a machine where physical laws completely determined everything that happened, then it is hard to see how there could be genuine free will or real scope for mental explanations as opposed to merely physical ones. Fortunately there is now good scientific evidence that this is not the case. (We discuss the question about the soul in more detail in appendix B.)

Let's come back to the soul. Your soul is your innermost being, the essence of "you"—not in some chemical or physical sense but in a spiritual sense. Here is another analogy: Imagine that there is a complex video game. It will contain various modules of software. There might be an operating system; there might be various rendering engines and all kinds of useful "utility software" that enables the game to be played. But there will also be some software that describes the specifics of the characters in the game. You could imagine that it is organized in a number of layers—appearance, muscles, and so forth. Of course the characters in a video game are only simulations, but if they were real people, the software would have to have an enormous number of layers (probably infinite, because of Gödel's theorem). At some point (we don't know where, but God does) the depth of these layers would be describing the person's innermost being. It's a bit like music, but the problem with the CD analogy that I have sometimes used is that a CD essentially has only one "layer," which is the digitization of the sound: it's much more like the score as opposed to the sound waves that the performers make, and even more like the essence of the music.

JP: The brain is far and away the most complicated physical system we have ever encountered in science's exploration of the physical world. It is certainly unpredictable in its future behavior. However, unpredictability is not necessarily the same as causal openness. As the philosophers say, the former is epistemological (what you can or cannot know), while the latter is ontological (what is actually the case). What connection you should make between the two is a matter for metaphysical question and cannot be settled by science alone (see question 6). For example, there are two alternative interpretations of quantum physics. One sees its unpredictabilities as simply arising from a degree of necessary ignorance about the details of an intrinsically deterministic physics. The other interpretation sees the unpredictabilities as a sign of actual indeterminism. Both theories give the same experimental predictions, so the choice between them cannot be made on scientific grounds alone.

If you are a realist, as most scientists are, you will want to make the connection between epistemology and ontology as close as possible. That is to say, you will believe that what we can or cannot know is a reliable guide to what is actually the case. That is why almost all physicists take the indeterministic view of quantum theory. I think that our basic human experiences of choice and responsibility should encourage us to believe that the brain is something much more subtle and supple than a mechanical device of immense complexity.

Science's knowledge of the causal structure of the world is also very patchy. For example, we do not fully understand how the subatomic quantum world relates to the apparently clear and reliable world of everyday physics. Chaos theory, which operates in the latter, is not reconcilable with quantum physics.

The latter has a scale, set by Planck's constant, while chaotic dynamics is fractal in character and so is scale free, the same all the way down. The two simply cannot be combined consistently. There is much more about these issues in chapter 2 of my *Exploring Reality.*

For my ideas about the soul, see chapter 9 of *The God of Hope and the End of the World.* It is a rather complex discussion, not satisfactorily reducible to a few words.

40. What Is Conscience?

What is conscience exactly? Is it that little voice inside of us, that gut feeling that guides us in choosing which course of action to take? Is it a little voice outside of us like Jiminy Cricket in Pinocchio? Is it a little of both, or is it neither? I know it's more than simply a gut feeling.

NB: I think the "exactly" is beyond the wit of man—or even of woman. Just as soul is our deepest self, so conscience is our deepest understanding of what is right and wrong. It may sometimes feel a bit like a "third party," but it isn't, although no doubt God can communicate with our conscience just as he can communicate with other aspects of our minds.

Of course, exactly how our minds relate to our brains and bodies is poorly understood, so it's too much to hope that conscience can be precisely understood. There are some suggestive PET images about parts of the brain that are associated with moral inhibitions, which are clearly related to, though not identical with, conscience.

JP: It is hard to understand, and even harder to deny, our deep inner experiences, such as conscience. I see its "voice" as part of the frontier of exchange between the human spirit and the Holy Spirit. I believe that we have real ethical knowledge. Our beliefs that love is better than hate, or that torturing children is wrong, are not simply survival strategies or conventions of our particular society. They are *facts* about the reality within which we live. Theism makes this intelligible for me, as it understands our ethical intuitions to originate as intimations of the good and perfect will of our Creator.

41. Does Human Life Have a Purpose?

*What do you make of the Harvard biologist E. O. Wilson's idea that "no species, ours included, possesses a purpose beyond the imperatives created by its own genetic history (i.e., evolution) . . . we have no particular place to go. The species lacks any goal external to its own biological nature" (*On Human Nature, *2–3). Surely, biological evolution is a scientific fact, but it only explains how we came to be. But should we base our entire worldview, including our view of morality, on it, as Wilson clearly does?*

NB: No, "genetic determinism"—in the sense that your genes inevitably determine your actions—is a nonsense that is not held by any serious scientists. Wilson of course does not hold this view either, but speaks of the extent to which our choices are constrained and influenced by our "genetic leash." Genes only act statistically—so they certainly *influence the probabilities* of certain outcomes, but they don't "program" you in a real sense. It is not even true that two people who have the same genome would always react the same if they were exposed to an identical environment. Identical twins, who do have essentially the same genome, may look very similar to outsiders, and the probability that they will have any given property tends to be strongly correlated. But as we have discussed in earlier responses, even if hypothetically two genetically identical humans were exposed from conception to *identical* stimuli from their environment, the indeterminacy of brain outcomes would mean that they would not react identically in all circumstances. In a sense, evolution is like gravity—it's a pervasive organizing principle but not the whole story.

Prof. Wilson is a distinguished scientist, but statements about "purpose" and "goals" immediately take you beyond the realms of science into metaphysical, philosophical, or theological territories: such statements are not susceptible to scientific investigation and are thus beyond his specific competence. It is clearly incorrect to say that no species has a goal external to its own biological nature in the sense that humankind has long intervened in evolution, originally by selective breeding and more recently by genetic engineering, in order to provide animals and plants for specific human purposes. Cultural factors are also highly significant in recent human evolution.

As for predictions of the triumph of scientific materialism, people have been saying such things since at least the 1790s. But over two hundred years of experience offers three interesting lessons.

Firstly, secular triumphalist regimes have been the biggest disasters and mass murderers in history: Mao, Stalin, and Hitler immediately spring to mind, and on a smaller scale—but only because he ruled over a smaller country—Pol Pot (Michael Burleigh is very good on the anti-religious nature of these regimes, starting with the French Revolution: see both his *Earthly Powers* and *Sacred Causes)*. Both Marxism and Nazism claimed to be based on science and were indeed supported by many of the scientific thinkers of their day. Darwin was very clear that his theories did *not* have the religious and social implications claimed by some of his followers, especially on the Continent, who saw his ideas as invaluable weapons in their fights against clericalism and Christianity. Dawkins, while of course happy to extol Darwinism for antireligious purposes, explicitly denounces Social Darwinism and takes great exception to the suggestion in *Darwin's Angel* that he "would have approved" of it. However, if it really were true that the only sources of morality or any other facts about human beings were Darwinian, then it is hard to see *from that point of view* why it is wrong to seek to eliminate "defective" genes and individuals from the gene pool, by lethal means if necessary

Secondly, the demise of religion never seems to happen on schedule. Even in the United Kingdom, which has a very secular culture in the commentariat, 72 percent of people in the 2000 census said they were Christian.

Finally, in biological and evolutionary terms, religion (esp. Christianity) appears to be good for you. Compared with secularists, Christians are happier, healthier, and have more grandchildren. By contrast, all over the world, secular societies appear to be committing demographic suicide, with birth rates significantly below replacement. Ironically, therefore, people who espouse the primacy of evolution in everything are adopting strategies that in their own terms are unsuccessful.

JP: The distinct personalities of identical twins show that absolute genetic determinism is untrue. The intricate structure of the individual brain is by no means completely genetically specified; instead, it develops in response to experience. For example, it is well known that the region of the brain that deals with spatial relationships is enlarged in London taxi drivers, who spend much time mastering the geography of the capital. Most of the structure of the brain is epigenetic (experience generated) rather than genetic. There are just not enough human genes to be able to program a system of such neural complexity.

42. Do Humans Matter More Than Animals?

Do you believe that humans have a higher status than other animals, and, if so, how is this arrived at through the process of evolution?

NB: Although humans are genetically surprisingly similar to other animals, we clearly have abilities and characteristics that not even our closest cousins the great apes possess. From a purely biological point of view, this is because what matters is not how many genes you have but how they are used in genetic circuits (*The Music of Life* by Denis Noble is very good on this). And in any complex system there are subtle thresholds that, when they are crossed, radically transform the system's behavior. Although we don't understand the details, it is clear that several of these thresholds have been crossed in human development: in particular the ability to use very rich and complex languages and, perhaps related to this, the ability to make deep moral and spiritual judgements.

The moment complex symbolic communication and language become major factors in the ability of individuals in a species to survive and reproduce, evolution takes on additional dimensions and can no longer be considered at a purely biological level. This is nicely explored in Jalbonka and Lamb's *Evolution in Four Dimensions,* and Martin Nowak's *Evolutionary Dynamics* summarizes some of the work in evolutionary dynamics in cultural evolution—a rapidly expanding field. From a theological point of view, the assertion that all human beings are made in the image of God is a statement that, contrary to some "Darwinian" views, all human beings matter equally and that genetic variations are, in a fundamental sense, irrelevant. Each human being is important enough to God for his son to die for.

So, yes, we do believe that human beings have higher status than animals. God has created us in his own image, using the wonderfully subtle and fruitful scientific principles that we are beginning to discern.

JP: Every so often in the history of the universe something intrinsically new emerges from within the deep potentiality with which creation has been endowed. This happened with the coming-to-be of life and again with the dawning of animal consciousness. I believe it also happened in the genus *Homo* with the emergence of human self-consciousness. The higher animals are conscious, of course, but they live only in the near present. The chimpanzee can figure out that if he throws up the stick, maybe the banana will fall down, but he does not brood on the knowledge that eventually he will die. We do. This intrinsic novelty of humanity raises interesting questions about the evolutionary process. Consider human mathematical abilities. For survival, we need not much more than counting and a little elementary geometry. Whence then has come the human ability to study noncommutative algebras and to prove Fermat's last theorem? I think that conventional Darwinian theory is unable to explain this capacity, which requires for its understanding the belief that our environment is not limited to the physical and biological but must also include contact with a noetic realm of mathematical ideas, into which our ancestors were increasingly drawn. These matters are extensively discussed in chapter 3 of my *Exploring Reality.*

I also believe that God interacts providentially with the unfolding history of creation in ways that respect the divine gift to creatures of the freedom to be themselves and "make themselves" through evolutionary process (see ch. 3 of my *Belief in God in an Age of Science,).*

Further Studies

Burleigh, Michael. 2005. *Earthly Powers: The Clash of Religion and Politics in Europe, from the French Revolution to the Great War.* New York: HarperCollins.

Burleigh, Michael. 2007. *Sacred Causes: The Clash of Religion and Politics, from the Great War to the War on Terror.* New York: HarperCollins.

Hefner, Philip. 2000. *The Human Factor: Evolution, Culture and Religion.* Theology and the Sciences. Minneapolis: Augsburg Fortress.

Murphy, Nancey, and Warren S. Brown. 2007. *Did My Neurons Make Me Do It? Philosophical and Neurobiological Perspectives on Moral Responsibility and Free Will.* Oxford: Oxford University Press.

Penrose, Roger. 2002. *The Emperor's New Mind: Concerning Computers, Minds, and the Laws of Physics.* Oxford: Oxford University Press.

Polkinghorne, John. 2005. *Exploring Reality: The Intertwining of Science and Religion.* London: SPCK.

7
Religion

43. Is Atheism a Form of Faith?

NB: The term *atheism* can be used in many different ways. Some atheists use it to mean "anyone who doesn't believe in God," thus sweeping up agnostics and anyone who has never considered the question. However, there are some people who appear to put their faith in particular flavors of atheism. Marxism, for example, clearly became a kind of faith system for many, both under communist dictatorships where it was promulgated with many of the trappings of a cult and in certain Western intellectual circles. People like Sartre, for example, openly compared their embrace of Marxism to a kind of religious conversion.

Even today one certainly comes across dogmatic atheists who appear to have a commitment to their positions that is well in excess of the "reason" that they ostensibly espouse. One way of detecting this is when people claim there is "no evidence whatsoever" for the existence of God. It is coherent to say there is "not enough evidence," which is what Bertrand Russell claimed he would say to God if he met him in the afterlife, but to claim that there is *no* evidence is intellectually indefensible. Such people will also deny, for purely ideological reasons, that religions offer any evolutionary benefits to their adherents, another manifestly false position (see appendix C for details). For some people atheism can provide an ideological underpinning for a whole range of important lifestyle choices involving sexual behavior and attitudes to relationships (Russell and Sartre would be prime examples), abortion, and business ethics. Jeff Skilling, the CEO of Enron, made it clear that *The Selfish Gene* was his favorite book. When Richard Dawkins found out about this after Enron collapsed, he expressed his mortification, and there is nothing in the science underpinning that book to justify fraudulent business practices. But an atheistic ideology that apparently places selfish competition at the heart of what it means to be human will naturally appeal to many people who have made a lot of money by competition in the marketplace.

The clear human need for some kind of faith can also lead to exaggerated emphasis on some prophets and seers of atheism, and a desire for sacred texts may partly explain the high sales of certain popular books. But in Christianity, at least, faith is a matter of love and a personal relationship, and there is no one at the heart of atheism that can take the place of God.

44. Can We See Truth?

Freud claims that we see everything through the tinted glass of perception. I feel that he carries this concept to extremes by implying that our "wish faculties" will always exceed our desire to see truth clearly and annihilate it. I would like to hear Dr. Polkinghorne or you rescue us from this dilemma of perception in our quest for pure "knowing," less relative to science than to theology and psychology.

NB: St. Paul knew, even better than Freud, that our perceptions of truth can be distorted by our hopes, fears, and earthly beliefs. John, as you know, espouses the approach of "critical realism," which suggests that we can get progressively more accurate understandings. "Scientists are mapmakers of the physical world. No map tells us all that could be conceivably be told" (*Faith, Science and Understanding*, ch. 5). John refers quite rightly to "the masters of suspicion . . . like Marx and Freud who claimed to reveal that human thought has its origin not in the ostensible objects of its engagement, but in the hidden motivations of class or sex" (*Scientists as Theologians*, 2) but who, of course, exempted their own thoughts from their critique. He contrasts this with the manifest success of critical realism in scientific matters. In summary, the fact that our perceptions are imperfect does not mean that they are always wrong, but merely that we have to adopt "the frame of mind where [we] may firmly hold to what [we] believe to be true, even though [we] know that it might conceivably be false" (*Faith, Science and Understanding*, 34, quoting Polanyi, *Personal Knowledge*, 214). And we must recognize that even for very good explanations, "there may be a significant element of modelling, at least in the way in which they express their insights in everyday language" (*Faith, Science and Understanding*, 84).

JP: All human knowing involves perception from a particular point of view, which will offer opportunities for insight but be bounded by its inherent limitations. I certainly do not think that this implies that we are unable to get beyond misleading tricks of perspective, but it does mean that we have to be careful. Nicholas quoted Michael Polyani (a very helpful writer on this subject), who emphasizes that science is precarious (it does not trade in unquestionable proof) but also reliable (it affords us verisimilitudinous knowledge). One place where you could find my take on this is chapter 2 of *Beyond Science*. I would extend this critical realism to theology also (see *Belief in God in an Age of Science*, chs. 2 and 5).

45. Which Stories in the Bible Are True?

Where, in relation to the Bible, does story end and history begin, and how can we tell the difference? I agree with John Polkinghorne about the nature of the creation stories in Genesis: surely, these narratives disclose foundational truths in the manner of, say, poetry or song. My question, however, concerns the dividing line biblical apologists draw between the first eleven chapters of Genesis and the supposedly historical accounts from Abraham onwards, including the Gospel traditions regarding Jesus. Many of the biblical stories are replete with delightful puns and allusions, yet they are embedded in texts that purport to be chronicles of Israel's history. If we convert the transfiguration into some kind of elaborate metaphor, why should we not feel compelled to do the same to the resurrection?

NB: For each part of the Bible, you have to ask what kind of writing it is and what God is trying to tell us through it. It is not a matter of poetry versus literal truth: we use notational conventions in science as well. For example, when I write $f = ma$, I don't mean to imply that the word "fry" means the same as the word "mary"—you have to understand when, and in what contexts, it is appropriate to substitute the symbols *ma* for the symbol *f*—and talk about the "big bang" does not imply cymbals and sound waves!

We cannot dismiss the first eleven chapters of Genesis as if myths were the same as fairy stories. Even though many of the exact details are not the point—as is clear from the fact that there are two creation stories in Genesis that differ in detail—God is saying, "Don't be hung up on the details; these are not important, but understand what I am trying to tell you about the fundamental truths about the relationships between God, humanity, and creation." This incidentally is why Darwin's theories were never rejected by the mainstream churches on theological grounds—in fact, he was buried in Westminster Abbey and the archbishops of Canterbury and York were on the committee for his funeral memorial.

Equally, Kings and Chronicles present somewhat different perspectives on the events they cover, and although they represent remarkable historiography for their time, we need to read the Scriptures in the light of Christ. And some of these books were written hundreds of years after the events they describe. However, when we come to the Gospels, we are dealing with serious attempts by eyewitnesses or people with direct access to them to tell the truth as it happened. The idea of the resurrection as an elaborate metaphor, for example, arose in the nineteenth century with people like Hegel and Strauss. But it's a nonsense: Jesus died and yet the tomb was empty (otherwise the Jewish and Roman authorities could have produced the body and nailed all this subversive talk of resurrection stone dead). So perhaps the disciples stole the body and fabricated the resurrection stories? Why would anyone give their lives for something they *knew* to be a lie?

It's not just Christian theology that implies that God can, and does, intervene in history. If God, a loving ultimate Creator, exists at all then he must interact with the creatures he loves from time to time. Of course, if you assume a priori that God does not exist, then it follows that God does not intervene in history—but atheism as a worldview poses serious difficulties. Perhaps this is why it has always been rather marginal and seems to be declining heavily worldwide after its brief and disastrous flowering in the twentieth century led to the worst regimes and human disasters in the whole of recorded history. Although there seems to be some increase in atheism in North America and Western Europe, this increase is vastly outweighed by the increase in religious belief in other parts of the world. There are probably 150–200 million Christians in China, up from perhaps 5 million during the Maoist era. Alister McGrath's book *The Twilight of Atheism* looks increasingly prescient, and the strident tone of books like *The God Delusion* rather reinforce that impression.

JP: The Bible is not a book but a library, with many kinds of writing, interweaving story and history. It is also important to figure out the genre of what one is reading. Poetry and prose are very different. When Robert Burns says his love "is like a red red rose," because it is poetry, we know he does not mean that his girlfriend has green leaves and prickles. When we read Genesis 1 we are not reading a scientific text but a deep theological discourse claiming that nothing exists except by the will of God ("And God said, 'Let there be . . .'"). When we read the Bible, we have to decide the nature of what we are reading at any one time. It is not surprising that there are some disagreements of detail between truth-seeking people about some points of the judgments involved. This is because subtle acts of discernment are involved in assessing genres, and there is no algorithm to the process.

46. How Does the Death of Jesus Save the World?

NB & JP: Christians believe that human beings have become alienated from God and that this relationship needs to be restored through our penitence and God's forgiveness. We also believe that Jesus Christ was both truly human (one of us) but also *Son* of God (divine). He is therefore the unique link between human life and divine life, the living means by which our relationship with God can be restored. It has been the witness of the church throughout the centuries that Christ's solidarity with us, even to the point of his painful and shameful death on the cross, is central to this process of restoration (atonement). Nevertheless, there has not been one single and universally accepted theory of exactly how this works. In science, we are familiar with the fact that there can be phenomena that cannot be denied but that are not wholly understood theoretically—quantum physics is a good example.

Perhaps one gains a little insight from recognizing that forgiveness is an intrinsically costly matter (it is not a question of just saying, "It doesn't matter") and that the lovingly accepted costliness of our salvation is manifested in the willingly accepted suffering of Christ.

47. Why Believe Jesus Rose from the Dead?

NB & JP: We have already sketched some of the serious evidential motivation for this counterintuitive belief (see our responses to questions 3 and 45). How one weighs that evidence will depend on wider considerations. A resolute skeptic can always maintain that nothing is so improbable as the resurrection, and so no evidence would ever be enough to support belief in it.

However, a Christian will see that there is a defensible case for believing that God's raising Jesus from the dead to live an unending life of glory is not the hasty act of a celestial conjurer but a rational consequence of who Jesus actually was. It is a vindication of the one whose life was not such that it could fittingly end in apparent failure. It is a vindication of the faithfulness of God, who did not abandon the one who wholly committed himself to trust in his heavenly Father. It is a vindication of the deep hope that lies in many human hearts, that the last word is not with death but with life. It is important to recognize that in Christian understanding, Jesus' resurrection is the guarantee and foretaste within history of a destiny that awaits all men and women beyond history. Paul told the Corinthians that "As in Adam all die, so also in Christ shall all be made alive" (1 Cor. 15:22).

48. How Much Do You Need to Believe to Be a Christian?

NB & JP: At the heart of Christian belief lie two mysterious, exciting, and, we believe, true ideas. One is the incarnation: God has acted to make the ineffable divine nature known in the clearest and most accessible way, by living the life of a man and dying a human death. Does the infinite God care for finite individuals? Did Jesus care for those in need who crossed his path? For the Christian the answer to the second question also answers the first.

The second central Christian belief is that of the Trinity. Trinitarian theology is deep and subtle, but its essential character is to recognize that the nature of the one true God is the eternal exchange of love between the three divine Persons. Christians believe that we know God in three ways: the Father (infinite Creator—God above us), the Son (God in human terms—God alongside us), and Holy Spirit (at work in our hearts—God within us). Yet there is one single divine Will at work in the wonderful and fruitful order of the world.

If God is love, surely God will have existed from all eternity in relationship. This is one of the truths revealed in the Trinity. It finds a pale reflection in what science is discovering about the intrinsic relationality of the physical and biological world. Although the approach of science has been largely reductionist, splitting things into component parts, we are increasingly realizing that this is only part of the story. Once two quantum entities have interacted with each other, they become mutually entangled so that acting on one will have an immediate effect on the other, however far away it may be. Even the subatomic world, it seems, cannot properly be treated atomistically.

49. What Place Do Non-Christians Have in God's Universe?

What place do atheists, Muslims, Jews, Buddhists, Hindus, and so on occupy in God's universe?

NB: God loves non-Christians—they are created in his image, and Jesus came to save us all. This seems clear from "And I, when I am lifted up from the earth, will draw all men [and women] to myself" (John 12:32). It's clear that some non-Christians are saved, and that God will save as many as he can. This makes John close to being a universalist.

I observe that if there is a probability $p > 0$ that someone will miss out on eternal loving union with God—an infinite good—through not truly embracing the Good News, then it doesn't matter what the value of p is, it is still infinitely important that they do so. And p must be > 0 because otherwise salvation is compulsory, and not an act of love.

This is an enormous topic, but it's worth looking at the sheep and the goats in Matthew 25:31–46. Of course, this is apocalyptic imagery, but we need to take it particularly seriously. The people of all nations will be gathered, and the Lord will separate them, not according to their stated beliefs but according to the extent to which they do the will of his Father who is in heaven by living in the way of love. Although it seems superficially that this is about "salvation by works," the point seems to be that these people have the right kind of faith, one that is alive and leads to action. For Jesus and indeed for the whole of the NT, "faith" is not "intellectual assent to propositions." As St. James says, "You believe that God is one; you do well. Even the demons believe—and shudder" (James 2:19). The justified go to "the kingdom prepared for you from the foundation of the world" (Matt. 25:34), but the condemned go to "the eternal fire prepared for the devil and his angels" (Matt. 25:41). The implication is that it is God's intention that everyone should be saved, and that those who reject his salvation are not going to a place of torment prepared for them but condemning themselves to a state that need not be theirs. The other clear implication is that although everyone is saved through Jesus Christ, not all are aware that they are being saved through him. The justified are astonished to find that they have been acting out of love for Jesus and ministering to him.

This is not to say that we should be complacent about the eternal destiny of those who consciously reject God's offer of salvation in Jesus. Even a small probability of missing out on an infinite good is a terrible risk. Nor can we limit the love of God. We must work out our own salvation with fear and trembling, for God is at work in us (Phil. 2:12–13), and judge not, that we may not be judged (Matt. 7:1; Luke 6:37).

JP: I believe that God has purposes for good and fulfillment for all creatures. I do not believe that any human being is outside the mercy and love of God, but equally no one will be carried into the kingdom of heaven against his or her will. Ultimately, all who will must come to the Father through Christ because he is the unique link between the life of God and the life of creation. However, this by no means implies that only those who have known Jesus by name in this life will be accepted. The love of God is not on offer for a limited period only.

I have discussed general issues of the relationships of Christianity to other faiths and to those of no faith at all in chapter 10 of my *Science and Christian Belief* (also known in North America as *The Faith of a Physicist).*

50. Will Sinners Suffer Eternal Punishment?

Christ speaks of eternal punishment, and regardless of whether he was using metaphor or speaking literally, the implication of some sense of awfulness succeeding death in certain cases is difficult to deny. What do you and Dr. Polkinghorne have to say about Christ's own words, perhaps most sharply in the tale of Lazarus and the rich man?

NB: There is a good report by the Doctrine Commission of the Church of England titled *The Mystery of Salvation* that grapples with these issues and to which John has contributed. My own take, for what little it's worth, is this. What do we know?

1. "God so loved the world"—he wants all humanity to be redeemed and through Jesus offers salvation as a free gift to everyone.
2. He has given us free will so that we have the power to choose. He will not force us to accept his love—he is not a rapist. It is pretty clear that God will save everyone whom he can—no one will be excluded because God did not want them.
3. The choice—loving union with God—yes or no—is of supreme importance. Compared with this no earthly loss even comes close—burning in fire, weeping, gnashing of teeth are pale approximations to the seriousness of the issue. They are clearly "picture language," but this does not mean that the reality is less, but that it is greater than words can adequately express.
4. We are not saved through our efforts or because we are any more "special" than the rest of humanity. The point that St. Paul is making in Romans 8 is that God is doing the work—not through our merits but through his love.
5. The faith that we need to show to appropriate God's free gift of salvation is not simply, or even primarily, intellectual assent to a series of propositions. Jesus says, "Not everyone who says to me, 'Lord, Lord,' shall enter the kingdom of heaven, but he who does the will of my

> Father who is in heaven" (Matt 7:21). This is not "justification by works" but a deep statement about the kind of thing that faith is. St. James of course makes the same point, that "faith without works is dead." For an interesting modern take on these issues see John Cottingham's *The Spiritual Dimension*.

So what of dives and Lazarus (Luke 16:19-31)? As with all the Bible, and especially the Gospels, it's worth seeing the passage in the wider context. Luke 16 begins with the "unjust steward," goes on with "you cannot serve God and mammon," a rebuke of "the Pharisees, who were lovers of money" and hard sayings about John and adultery, before this culminating story. Well, it is a parable and not all the details are *necessarily* significant. It's partly a story against the idea that riches are God's blessing and poverty God's curse, and partly a warning that we should use riches in this life to relieve poverty. But the main point is that Jesus, in his resurrection, is the fulfillment of the Scriptures. Another point that would have been obvious to people in the first century but that needs explaining today is that Dives is one of *six* brothers: seven symbolizes perfection. The resurrection makes perfect what "Moses and the prophets" point to. Note also that Dives's "altruism" only extends to his kin. But Abraham never says that no one will believe, merely that some will not, partly because they have already hardened their hearts and not listened to God's Word. As for "the great gulf fixed" we know that Jesus "descended into Hell" and that he was strong enough to break the power of death (see, e.g., Matt. 27:52–53).

We need to set this parable in the context of everything else that Jesus taught, and perhaps especially relevant are the "sheep and the goats" (see 7.49).

What we must never do, of course, is look down on "them" as the "nonelect," since it is God's will that we should do everything we can to encourage others to accept the gift of salvation, and even St. Paul was not prepared to take his own salvation for granted.

JP: I do not think everyone's eternal destiny is fixed at death—think of those whose geographical or historical situation prevented their hearing the gospel, of those whose response has been crippled by experiences like child abuse. Yet wittingly to turn from Christ in this life is spiritually dangerous, and I think that is what the stern NT language about judgment is principally intended to convey. For a more detailed discussion see *The God of Hope and the End of the World*, esp. chapter 11.

51. What Is the Point of Praying?

Is the reason for prayer praise, thanksgiving, forgiveness, redemption, change? If your prayers are a request for change (e.g., an end to war or famine, a cure for an illness, help with exams, etc.), I have trouble understanding the reasoning behind such requests in light of your statement that "God chooses to limit his omniscience as well as his omnipotence." Do you believe that he limits his omniscience/omnipotence only partially, in which case some requests (but very few) may get answered; or do you believe he limits these powers totally, in which case prayer specifically for change, although very common, would be pointless (apart, perhaps, from the solace of the person saying the prayers)?

NB & JP: We do both pray, and our prayers include intercessory prayers, and following the example of Jesus' prayers, they are implicitly qualified with "nevertheless, not my will, but thy will be done." We don't quite know what it would mean for God to limit his power totally—it would be a deist conception whose coherence we rather doubt, and certainly not the God of the Bible. God limits himself out of love and to the extent that love requires: of course we don't understand the details of this, but the principle seems clear. The God whose nature is love can be neither a deistic spectator just watching it all happen in isolated indifference nor a cosmic tyrant whose creation is a puppet theater in which the divine puppeteer pulls every string. The Christian God will interact with creatures without overruling them in some arbitrary fashion. One can pray to such a

God, but to do so with integrity implies opening oneself to a willingness to cooperate with the divine Will. In prayer we are called to clarify our deepest desires. John has discussed these issues in more detail in *Science and Providence.*

Further Studies

Cottingham, John. 2005. *The Spiritual Dimension.* Cambridge: Cambridge University Press.

McGrath, Alister. 2004. *The Twilight of Atheism: The Rise and Fall of Disbelief in the Modern World.* New York: Doubleday.

Polkinghorne, John. 1994. *Science and Christian Belief: Theological Reflections of a Bottom-Up Thinker.* London: SPCK.

Ward, Keith. 1994. *Religion and Revelation: A Theology of Revelation in the World's Religions.* Oxford: Oxford University Press.

Wright, Tom. 2006. *Simply Christian: Why Christianity Makes Sense.* New York: HarperCollins.

8
Conclusion

> "There is nothing new to be discovered in physics now. All that remains is more and more precise measurement."
>
> Lord Kelvin (1900)

Kelvin was a great scientist and a highly intelligent man. Although in this statement he was completely mistaken, it did not seem unreasonable to most people at the time. The difficulties of reconciling electromagnetism and Newtonian mechanics, which led to the theory of relativity, seemed fairly minor, and no one could have realized that the photoelectric effect (which was not really described until 1901) would, with the Nobel Prize-winning insight of Einstein in 1905, unleash the whole quantum revolution. Sometimes an event that seems insignificant at the time to most people can change the whole of history: such as the birth of a particular child around 6 BC.

The more we know, the more interesting questions we can ask. One difference between wisdom and mere knowledge is that wisdom deepens your understanding of how much you don't know. It was only possible for Einstein to ask the questions that led to his theories of relativity because of the work of Newton and Maxwell on gravity and electromagnetism. Questions about the extraordinary zoo of subatomic particles only become possible once one has "split the atom"—a concept that would once have seemed a contradiction in terms. And it is only once you have good enough theories of the origin of the universe that you can begin to be amazed by the anthropic fine-tuning we discussed in chapter 3.

In addition to the specific points we have discussed, we have tried to dispel a number of misconceptions. For example, we hope that readers, whether or not they agree with all our points, will see that there are strong reasons for thinking the following:

1. It is not irrational to believe in God. It is logically possible that belief in God is mistaken—but it is certainly not a "delusion."
2. There is no real conflict between science and Christianity, though there are puzzles about how they relate to each other, as there are similar puzzles about the relationship between the different sciences.
3. The idea that most objects in the universe are machines is fundamentally mistaken, especially when applied to human beings. In particular, science does not require us to believe that we do not have free will.

But there is another, perhaps even more damaging and fundamental misconception that we wish to dispel. We might call it the territorial idea of knowledge—that there is a limited territory of knowledge and, like some nineteenth-century imperialist, science needs to "advance" by "pushing back ignorance and superstition" until eventually the whole of the map is painted red, or whatever national color appeals. This is deeply flawed in two main respects. First, there are always many levels of understanding, and the imperialist tendency to suggest that things are "nothing but atoms and molecules" simply diminishes understanding: the *Mona Lisa* and the Grand Canyon are indeed composed of atoms and molecules but are certainly a great deal more than the sum of them.

Second, potential knowledge is not a finite domain. Each advance in understanding leads to more questions to be asked and more fascinating detail to explore. A deeper understanding of the chemistry, geology, hydrology, and ecology of the Grand Canyon need not, in any way, diminish the beauty, awe, wonder, and poetry that we experience. Science, properly understood, does not explain away the other aspects of the phenomena in question but can deepen their possibilities. With appropriate humility and realism about the limitations of human understanding and wisdom, there is no limit to the territory that can be explored.

The explorations are fascinating, and we hope that the responses we have offered have helped readers advance in their own journeys—however much, or little, they agree with what we have said. We have certainly had our understandings deepened and broadened in writing this book.

The sky remains blue. There are clouds, winds. Perhaps indeed they have been diverted by a butterfly flapping its wings. Beyond the atmosphere, planets, meteors, stars, black holes: they too are subject to chaotic dynamics, ultimately impossible to predict in complete detail. As is your brain—by far the most complex system of which we are aware. Machines, even the most beautiful and elegant, are only a fraction of the universe. But the whole of the universe is teeming with matter and energy—dark and otherwise—and is amazingly finely tuned to carry within it the potential for intelligent life. Behind this, some see nothing: others discern the mind, and the love, of God.

Appendix A
Anthropic Fine-Tuning

In this appendix we outline some of the points about anthropic fine-tuning in somewhat greater detail. For a more comprehensive treatment the reader is urged to consult the references. To make this appendix self-contained we are repeating much of the material in our responses to questions 20 and 21 in chapter 3 but adding more details. Martin Rees's book *Just Six Numbers* gives an excellent overview of the topic, and while we don't fully agree with his conclusions, we have nothing but admiration for his science.[1]

OUTLINE

Anthropic fine-tuning is a big topic that has been explored extensively, but the basic idea is easy to grasp. Imagine for a moment that we know the fundamental laws of nature, and suppose that these are in some sense responsible for generating the universe. It is highly likely that there will be some fundamental numbers that have to be plugged into these laws in order to get the universe we actually live in. As far as we know at present there are at least[2] six such numbers:

1. The number N is the ratio of the strength of the electrical forces that hold atoms together to the strength of gravity. It is about 10^{36} (1 with 36 zeros after it or 1,000,000,000,000,000,000,000,000,000,000,000,000).
2. Epsilon (ε) defines how firmly atomic nuclei bind together. It is about 0.007.
3. Omega (Ω) measures the amount of material in our universe and gives the relative importance of gravity and expansion energy. Its present value seems to be somewhere between 0.3 and 1. However, for Ω to be in this range now, then, according to the laws of physics as currently understood, in the early universe (say one second after the big bang) Ω would have had to be between 0.999999999999999 and 1.000000000000001—that is, within 1 part in 10^{15} of 1.
4. Lambda (Λ) controls the acceleration of the long-range expansion of the universe in general telativity. Its value is about 10^{-120}. Einstein actually thought that introducing Λ was his "greatest blunder"[3] and that it should have been left out (which would have been equivalent to setting it to zero by definition), but very careful measurements have shown that it is in fact slightly positive. It is now usually referred to as "dark energy."
5. The number Q represents the ratio of two fundamental energies (the gravitational energy required to pull galaxies apart and the energy corresponding to their mass, by Einstein's famous formula $e = mc^2$). It is about 10^{-5}.
6. The constant D is the number of space-like dimensions in our universe. Kant thought it was a necessary truth that this number was 3, but it turns out to be an empirical question. Einstein of course introduced the idea of time as a further dimension. String theorists suggest that space-time may have as many as eleven or more dimensions.

There are alternative ways of formulating some of these constants. For example, N is often thought of in terms of the gravitational fine structure constant α_G (whose value is about 5.906×10^{-39}) and the electrical fine structure constant α (whose value is about 1/137).

It turns out that if any of these numbers were appreciably different from their presently observed values, not only would there be no life on Earth but there would, as far as anyone can tell, be no prospect of intelligent life *anywhere* in the universe. To give a rough idea of how accurate this "fine-tuning" needs to be, ε has to be about 0.007 rather than about 0.006 or 0.008, and the early universe value of Ω has to be 1 to within about 1 part in 10^{15}. The constant Λ has to be almost exactly zero, to within one part in 10^{100}. And there are strong arguments that if there were anything other than three macroscopic space-like dimensions, intelligent life would be impossible.

It is beyond the scope of this appendix to go into the details of why these parameters have to take values very close to the observed values—this is ably discussed in the literature[4] and accepted by all competent physicists who have considered the problem. But let's consider just one example. If N were slightly higher, all stars would be blue giants, and if it were slightly lower, all stars would be red dwarfs. Because red dwarfs don't explode to make supernovae, there would be no second-generation stars and no carbon, oxygen, and so on available to make life on planets. And blue giants have lifetimes of the order of tens or hundreds of millions of years, which is much shorter than the four billion years or so that seem to be required for the evolution of intelligent life. There is also reason to suspect that blue giants would not have planets.[5]

No one knows what the possible range of these numbers actually is. Indeed, if there is only one universe, it is difficult to be sure what "the possible range of these numbers" would actually mean. But there is no obvious reason that the known laws of physics wouldn't work if N were (say) 100 and ε were (say) 42. It is even harder to know what the right probability distributions for the possible values of these parameters should be.[6] But pretty well every competent physicist who has looked into this finds these coincidences remarkable.

Consider just the value of Ω; what does it mean to be "1 to within about 1 part in 10^{15}"? Well, imagine you are making a sponge cake and the recipe calls for equal quantities of flour and granulated sugar. A grain of sugar is about 600 Ìm across, so to get a quantity of granulated sugar right to within one part in 10^{15} you'd need 10^{15} such grains, which would be equivalent to about 180,000 tons of sugar. Or suppose you are putting a golf ball. A hole must be 108 mm in diameter, and the ball has to be 42.67 mm in diameter, so let us say for simplicity that you have to get the ball within 100 mm of the center of the hole. The world record hole-in-one distance is apparently 448 yards, or 410 meters. So the best hole-in-one has an accuracy of about one part in 4100. One part in 10^{15} would be getting a hole-in-one from 10^{11} km away—which is about thirteen times the maximum distance from Earth to Pluto.

The situation is even more extreme with early-universe Λ's having to be so close to zero. Getting the sugar right to within one part in 10^{100} would be like an accuracy of one grain in a mass of 1.8×10^{95} tons of sugar, and the mass of the sun is only 2×10^{27} kg. And remember, there is no known reason, other than the emergence of intelligent life, why these constants should be related.

FOUR POSSIBILITIES

So to explain anthropic fine-tuning, there are essentially four possibilities:

1. This fine-tuning is highly unlikely in a random possible universe, but God has ensured in his loving wisdom that it is so, so that we can come into being.
2. This fine-tuning is highly unlikely in a random possible universe, but just by luck the one that exists is anthropic.
3. This fine-tuning is highly unlikely in a random possible universe, but there are such a vast number of other universes that it is not unlikely that at least one of them is anthropic.

4. There are as yet undiscovered reasons why this fine-tuning is not highly unlikely in a random possible universe.

It's fair to say that pretty well all atheists with a scientific background who have seriously considered the matter are driven to accept possibility 3 and explicitly to avoid possibility 1, and with very little other scientific motivation. Possibility 2 is just too much of a cop-out. If the string/brane theorists are on the right lines, and we are in a ten- or eleven-dimensional space-time and not a four-dimensional one, the chances are that there will be *extra* constants that are mysteriously fine-tuned, not fewer. Option 4 would arguably be the most remarkable coincidence.

There is a lot of debate about the philosophical and meta-scientific significance of anthropic fine-tuning. Clearly, we can only raise the question because we are here, but such a remarkable number of coincidences surely demand to be made intelligible by some deeper explanation. Some cosmologists propose that it is the anthropic property that selects this universe to be actualized from the almost infinite number of other possible universes. But this is clearly not a scientific argument in the normal sense of "materialist" science. Stephen Hawking argues that you need a "top-down cosmology" based on anthropic reasoning to understand the observed state of the universe. In particular, he suggests that almost all the landscapes postulated by string theory are nonanthropic. As he says, "A bottom-up approach to cosmology either requires one to postulate an initial state of the universe that is carefully fine-tuned—as if prescribed by an outside agency—or it requires one to invoke the notion of eternal inflation, a mighty speculative notion to the generation of many different universes, which prevents one from predicting what a typical observer would see."[7]

WHAT ABOUT INFLATION?

A concept called "inflation" in cosmology, which is currently widely accepted, proposes that in the early universe there was an inflationary epoch where an inflation field caused an exponential increase in the size of the very early universe. The main motivation for this proposal is to account for the remarkable fine-tuning of Ω. By adjusting the parameters of inflation (in the simplest models there are just two parameters), you can get a close match to observed values of Ω and to the levels of fluctuations in the early universe from which Q can be derived.

Although most cosmologists currently believe in some version of inflation, there are some quite serious difficulties. For one thing, the idea of inflation predicts the existence of a particle, called the inflaton, which has not been observed and whose mass, according to the principles of the standard model, should probably be such that it would be readily observable. How and, indeed, whether inflation occurs is very much an open question—it is one of the (many) hopes of theorists that string theory will deliver some answers to this perplexing problem.[8] However, string theory in its present state of development is so incomplete and has so many "free" parameters that the extent of anthropic fine-tuning required is pretty well unbounded. Indeed, many string theorists regard anthropic arguments as the only way to explain which of the immense number of possible theories and parameter sets actually occurs. Other approaches, such as quantum loop gravity, offer their own suggested explanations of the fact that Ω is so near 1.

Inflation also has a number of interesting side effects. It tends to imply that the universe is much bigger than we can know, and in some versions it "creates" a vast number of additional universes that in some ways resemble a foam at the edge of the universe we know.

It is not our purpose to argue that inflation does not occur—maybe it does or maybe there is some other mechanism that will turn out to explain the values of some of the key parameters we mentioned. But we note that inflation, if it does occur, doesn't eliminate the fine-tuning problem: to explain two observable parameters, it introduces a complicated theoretical mechanism with vast unobservable cosmological implications that itself needs at least two parameters to have the right values. At a fundamental level, the mystery remains.

DAWKINS

Let us now look at the proposed rebuttals to anthropic fine-tuning that Richard Dawkins offers in *The God Delusion*. Like most biologists of his generation, Dawkins does not appear to be comfortable with detailed calculations. In his discussion of the anthropic principle he offers two attempted rebuttals: First, he suggests that it "can be answered by the suggestion . . . that there are many universes," and then he discusses some variants of this idea.[9] He also suggests that "any God capable of designing a universe, carefully and foresightfully tuned to lead to our evolution, must be a supremely complex and improbable entity who needs an even bigger explanation than the one he is supposed to provide."[10]

MULTIVERSE AND ITS VARIANTS

Answering an argument by a suggestion is hardly conclusive. One problem is that we don't just need a hundred other universes, or even a billion, but an utterly immense number—some string theorists suggest that there are up to 10^{500} other universes. If you are allowed to posit 10^{500} other universes to explain away otherwise inconvenient observations, you can "explain away" anything, and science becomes impossible.

This is not to say that multiverse ideas are necessarily wrong—God's creation is amazing and full of surprises. At present the multiverse idea is pretty popular with cosmologists, mainly because it "explains" fine-tuning but also because it fits in well with ideas like inflation and string theory, which are the staple diet of most theoretical cosmology. At present it appears that there are so many free parameters in such theories that some form of "fine-tuning" would almost certainly exist, although these theories are not yet defined well enough for any such work to be done. It is currently standard in string theory to consider the concept of a "landscape" of string theories, which are "selected" by some form of anthropic principle, although this approach has been strongly criticized. Christians would of course affirm that if a multiverse existed, God would be its Creator and all lovable beings within it would be recipients of his love.[11]

Dawkins also advocates the "serial big crunch" model: the idea that the universe might expand and contract and then expand again with slightly different parameters, thus eventually having the right set of values. He is half-hearted about this idea but apparently doesn't realize that it is nonviable. If any universe generated expands forever or fails to expand at all, the series would terminate, and both these possibilities are quite likely. In a nutshell there are two problems, only one of which Dawkins seems to realize.

He says that "recent evidence is starting to steer us away from the big crunch model. It now looks as though our own universe is destined to expand forever," for which there is now strong evidence, especially since Λ appears to be fractionally greater than 0. But an elementary calculation shows that if the probability that a "random" set of constants would lead to an infinitely expanding universe is p, then the expected number of generations in this hypothetical "serial big crunch" model is $1/p$.

A more subtle problem is that although solutions for such bouncing cosmologies have been found in various approximations, it has been shown, using several different techniques, that solutions of this kind are unstable. In particular, one finds that generic, small perturbations at early times (or merely taking into account the remaining degrees of freedom) dramatically change the evolution near the transition. Rather than evolving towards an expanding semiclassical universe at late times, one generically produces a strong curvature singularity.[12]

COSMOLOGICAL NATURAL SELECTION?

Dawkins also likes Lee Smolin's idea of cosmological natural selection, which we'll call CNS. This idea suggests that:

1. Universes might be "born" mainly from black holes in other universes,

2. There might be small random variations in their fundamental constants, and
3. The fine-tuning of the parameters required for life might also sharply maximize the production of black holes.

Given these assumptions, and a few others, the probability that a random universe in the hypothetical multiverse was anthropic would be quite high. Dawkins, alas, obscures the highly conjectural nature of these assumptions, each of which is implausible. There are also serious problems with CNS from the perspective of evolutionary dynamics.[13]

Point one requires *not only* that black holes act as "universe creation machines" *but also* that there are no other significant universe creation mechanisms, such as "eternal inflation,"[14] which has rather more theoretical backing—although there is certainly no firm evidence of either. Inflation is pretty widely accepted by cosmologists, who point to its success in explaining the distribution of the Cosmic Background Radiation. But the fields and particles predicted by inflation have not been detected, and the indirect evidence seems completely insufficient to justify the enormous inferences that are drawn—e.g., that even if the initial size of the inflationary universe were as small as the Planck scale, $l_p \sim 10^{-33}$ cm, after 10^{-30}s of inflation this acquires a huge size of $10^{1,000,000,000,000}$ cm—and the prediction of "an infinite 'ergodic' space which contains Hubble volumes realizing all initial conditions—including one with an identical copy of you about $10^{10\wedge 29}$m away."[15] The idea that "inside" every black hole there is another universe also has some theoretical support, but there are several problems[16] and no possibility of experimental confirmation. In addition the number of black holes in our universe seems to be well in excess[17] of 10^{11} and if each of these has a universe with black holes (and so on) we have "conjured up" an exponentially unbounded number of unobserved universes. To us the willingness of cosmologists to make mind-boggling postulates in order to explain the anomalous fine-tuning of various observed parameters has something of the flavor of epicycles—and also makes the alleged scholastic debates about the number of angels that can dance on a pinhead appear restrained and parsimonious in comparison. Indeed a fundamental problem with all of these ideas is that they are extrapolating imperfectly understood physics to energy scales many many orders of magnitude above those at which they have been experimentally verified. As we have noted earlier, the whole history of science shows that this kind of extrapolation is unlikely to be valid—cosmologists are famously "often in error but seldom in doubt." As acts of scientific and mathematical exploration these speculations are, of course, entirely legitimate. But nonspecialists can get the impression that these are "scientific facts" rather than theoretical speculations that will almost certainly turn out to be wrong.

Point two is highly conjectural, and seems to violate one of the few "known" facts about black holes, which do not swallow up information as was first thought to be the case.[18] Lee[19] offers some theoretical arguments that black holes (may) bounce and that quantum effects could remove the singularity to our past, implying that there was something to the past of our big bang, although these "results" depend on a particular theory of "loop quantum gravity" that is controversial and far from proven. There is also the serious problem of what probability distributions to use for the variations in the parameters. In general a probability distribution for the variation of k parameters needs at least k new parameters to describe it, and often considerably more. Although in evolutionary dynamics many different distributions will lead to the same results, it is essential for CNS that none of the random variations in the parameters is large compared to the range of anthropic fine tuning. Otherwise even if the *expected* value of the parameter in question is exactly right, the *probability* that you will get that value or near enough can be vanishingly small. For example, if the anthropic value of Λ is between (say) 0 and 10^{-120} then if the random variations in Λ were about 1 the chance of a random universe having Λ in the required range would still be about 10^{-120} (depending of course on the distribution) even if this was the "expected" outcome.

On the point about maximizing black hole production, Lee makes a case that some of the possible variations in parameters would reduce this—not nearly enough is known about all the processes involved to be certain. However it seems that our universe is about a factor of 10,000 away from being maximally loaded with black holes, and even a 10 percent change in the spectral index of primordial fluctuations would fill the early universe with collapsed objects.[20] There is also the problem, as Lee admits, that in the very long run another mechanism of black hole creation which depends only on Λ being positive could well dominate the production of black holes by the mechanisms that CNS needs.[21]

So what of the problems from an evolutionary dynamics perspective? Well firstly, it is not enough for this idea to work that the number of black holes is *maximized* in the anthropic case; it has to be *maximized so sharply* that the probability of an anthropic universe is high (we touched on this a bit in the discussion of Λ above). A simple example may help illustrate the point. If I toss a fair coin four times and get exactly two heads, it is not very surprising: not only is it the most likely outcome but the probability is 37.5 percent. But if I toss it a thousand times and get exactly five hundred heads, although this is still the "most probable" *single* outcome, the probability is only 2.5 percent, and with a million tosses the probability of getting exactly 500,000 heads is minute.

Another very serious set of difficulties concerns the time and generations involved. In evolutionary dynamics we look at a population evolving over time. It is very unclear whether there is a satisfactory way in which you can place an ensemble of universes generated in this way in a relation to each other so that Lee can meaningfully talk about the population at time *t*. Lee originally suggested that we could work with "generation number" as *t*, but some universes (especially with $\Lambda > 0$) have an infinite lifetime and keep on producing black holes indefinitely. They would therefore have an infinite number of descendants in a finite "evolutionary time" and the whole framework of evolutionary dynamics collapses.[22] Lee accepts that this is a serious problem, and is working actively on concepts of time in quantum gravity, including a book project with the remarkable Brazilian philosopher Roberto Mangabeira Unger.

So let's suppose this "multiversal time" problem can be solved. Some possible universes have a much shorter lifetime than others, and what matters in evolution is not the number of children you have but the rate of increase in your descendants over time. Consider a "mayfly" that lives for 1 year and has 2 children and a "tortoise" that lives for 100 years and has 20 children, one every 5 years. The tortoise maximizes Lee's "fitness function" but (in the absence of other constraints) the mayflies will vastly outnumber tortoises.[23] Similarly a "mayfly" universe that only had two daughter universes but lasted for one year, would vastly out-compete a universe that produced 10^{20} daughter universes after about 10 billion years, since by that time there would be $2^{10,000,000,000}$ (about $10^{3,000,000,000}$) daughter "mayflies." Lee's initial response to this point was that we don't know if there are any possible universes which produce two black holes after one year. But collapsing universes can have arbitrarily short lifetimes and can produce plenty of black holes. In addition, nothing so extreme as one year is needed: a universe that produced two black holes after one million years would still do the trick. Not remotely enough is known about the dynamics of the production of black holes as a function of the varying basic parameters of physics for meaningful calculations to be done.[24]

There is also a problem of profligacy. In evolutionary dynamics we typically consider 10^n generations where n is something between 2 and 8. If most universes have about 10^{11} "daughters" (Lee would suggest even more) this would require us to consider something between $10^{1,100}$ and $10^{1,100,000,000}$ universes in our population. This makes the 10^{200} (or 10^{500}) or so possible "string theories" seem modest and restrained by comparison.

Lee is careful to claim that we are at a local maximum for the production of black holes and not necessarily that we are at a global maximum. If this is true (there is some debate) it is an interesting observation, whether or not the CNS arguments work. A theist would not be surprised if God had optimized the universe for life, and not merely made life possible.[25] But in the absence of resource or other constraints the relative frequencies of the "species" at the global maximum versus that at the local maximum will grow exponentially, and so the "solution" offered to anthropic fine-tuning won't work. Natural selection depends on having finite resources for which members of a population must compete, and there is no reason to think that the same applies with the profligate (hypothetical) creation of universes. Positing suitable constraints should repair some of the holes in Lee's theory, but of course this raises the question of why *these* constraints were chosen. Indeed, unless it turns out to be *logically necessary* that the universe/multiverse has the properties that Lee needs (which is wildly implausible), we would still be left with the remarkable anthropic coincidence that the universe happened to have just those properties that enabled "cosmological natural selection" to produce anthropic universes. So even if the physics and evolutionary dynamics can be made to work, which is highly doubtful, it seems that CNS is at best an example of what Nicholas calls the exploding free parameter postulate: a theory that seeks to explain the fine-tuning of the standard model eventually has more free parameters than are explained.

To be fair, Lee advocates CNS to demonstrate the possibility of developing a genuinely scientific theory about why the universe is likely to be anthropic—one that makes specific predictions that can, in principle, be falsified.[26] This is part of his argument against string theory, which he thinks is in danger of becoming nonscience because it is unfalsifiable. He is not primarily quarrelling with the theological anthropic principle (though he does not in fact accept it)—but with the misapplication, as he sees it, of anthropic arguments to salvage the inordinate prolixities of string theory and multiverses. It is highly commendable that he offers specific falsifiable predictions and engages in detail with the actual physics of black hole formation. Whether or not his ideas are right, his pursuit of them, in the teeth of a fashionable consensus, is admirable. But they certainly don't amount to a refutation of the type of anthropic principle in which we are interested.

A COMPLEX AND IMPROBABLE GOD?

Let's now deal with the second of Dawkins's objections, which is that God must be complex and is hence "improbable." There are many confusions here, and it is hard to know where to begin.

First of all, this objection confuses three types of complexity: complexity of specification, complexity of nature, and complexity of implications. Consider for a simplified example a right-angled triangle two of whose sides have length 1. The length of the third side is of course $\sqrt{2}$. This is a highly "improbable" number that in decimal form consists of an infinite, nonrepeating sequence of digits. But it is simple to specify. Furthermore, if the triangle in question is made of some suitably exotic material (perhaps some nanomaterial carefully arranged to be a catalyst), then the actual nature of the third side of this triangle could be difficult to specify precisely. Nevertheless, you can make precise and simple statements about its length, using the simple *concept* of $\sqrt{2}$, and indeed from this you could make specific and useful predictions, such as the rate at which this catalyst would work.

In much of science we use theories that are fairly simple to specify but have mind-bogglingly complex implications. You can literally write down the Einstein equation (for general relativity) on a postage stamp. Here it is:

$$R_{ab} - \frac{1}{2} R g_{ab} = -8\pi T_{ab} + \Lambda g_{ab}.$$

The variable Λ (lambda) is our old friend the cosmological constant previously discussed. The other mysterious symbols refer to certain fields that, according to general relativity, exist everywhere in space and time: the Ricci tensor (R_{ab}), the scalar curvature (R), the metric tensor (g_{ab}), and the stress-energy tensor (T_{ab}). The details of what these are don't matter for the present discussion, so this equation can be stated pretty simply. But the implications, and the solutions are of extraordinary complexity: in most cases no exact solutions can be found.

Its cousin the Dirac equation does much the same job for quantum theory. It can be written down very simply as

$$(\gamma^{\mu}\partial_{\mu} + im)\psi = 0$$

Again, the meaning of these symbols is complex, and for the present purposes the details are beside the point. It assumes the existence of a quantum wave-function ψ that is defined at every point of space and time (and for various spin states) on which certain mathematical operations, γ^{μ} and ∂_{μ}, can be performed and for which there is a quantity (m) that is the "rest mass" of the particle in question.

These equations are universally used by physicists, and although people are trying to come up with a comprehensive theory that integrates general relativity and quantum theory, everyone agrees that these two equations give enormously accurate accounts of a wide range of physical phenomena, and so far they have withstood very accurate experimental testing. They come as close as any equations could to "explaining" the behavior of matter. But by Dawkins's "argument" we should reject both equations without even doing experiments because "anything that offers such an explanation must be supremely complex and improbable." We agree of course that it is remarkable that such simple and beautiful equations seem to describe so much about the universe—one that is explained by the existence of a loving ultimate Creator and left wholly unexplained by Dawkins and his atheist colleagues.

Now, let's look at the comparable assertion to the Einstein equation that Christians make: There exists a loving ultimate Creator who has revealed himself in Jesus of Nazareth. The comparable assertion for Judaism might be "There exists a loving ultimate Creator revealed in the (Hebrew) Bible." We have here a simple *specification* even though the *implications* are astonishingly complex and wonderful. Of course, to understand this assertion you need explanations of the terms used, but this also applies to the highly complex symbols and entities in the Einstein and Dirac equations.

At this point Dawkins or his defenders might object that he is not saying that the *assertion* of the existence of God is complex but that *God* is complex. However, both the Einstein and

Dirac equations implicitly assert the existence of highly "complex" entities (the space-time manifold and the quantum vacuum), but the point is that they can be specified simply. If this "argument" of Dawkins against the existence of God were valid, then it would also be a valid argument against all of fundamental physics.

In addition a couple of Dawkins's points apply specifically to God. The first is the doctrine of divine simplicity. Dawkins has at least heard of this idea, though having attributed the bizarre view to Richard Swinburne that "God constantly keeps a finger on each and every particle,"[27] he then goes on to assert, "A God capable of continuously monitoring and controlling the individual status of every particle in the universe *cannot* be simple."[28] He gives no justification for this view, which seems to rest on the assumption that God gets his knowledge and exercises his powers the same way we do, via brains, computers, instruments, or other complex physical entities. But no serious theist suggests this—and, as Swinburne says, whether a hypothesis is simple or not is an intrinsic feature of that hypothesis, not a matter of its relation to observable data. Again, to take an analogy from physics, it is thought that the Higgs field in some sense gives mass to all the particles in the universe. If this were a theological entity, Dawkins might describe it as "keeping a finger on each and every particle" and conclude that the Higgs field is "too complex." It is an exciting and currently open question whether or not the Higgs field actually exists—most physicists think it does, and the hope is that the new facility at CERN called LHC will settle the question by observing the Higgs particle that is thought to mediate this field. Most people think the Higgs particle will turn out to exist, in which case a Nobel Prize is almost certain for the brilliant physicist Peter Higgs,[29] who proposed it in 1964—but perhaps it will not. But no serious scientist or philosopher is deterred from believing in the Higgs field by considerations such as those advanced by Dawkins.

The second is a simpler point: Christians, Jews, and Muslims assert the existence of an Ultimate Creator. To ask, "Who created the Ultimate Creator?" or "What explains the Ultimate Creator?" is simply to show that you have not understood the meaning of the term. From a philosophical point of view, an Ultimate Creator might or might not exist, but unless you can show that the concept of an Ultimate Creator is genuinely *logically impossible*—and even Dawkins doesn't think that this is the case—you cannot meaningfully ask for an explanation of the Ultimate Creator's existence.

Part of the theological meaning of divine simplicity is that in God, essence and existence coincide, so that the deity is a self-sustaining Being with no need for reliance on any other source of origin.

These topics, and other difficulties with Dawkins's excursions from science into philosophy, are ably discussed in Keith Ward's *Why There Almost Certainly Is a God.*

POSTSCRIPT ON IMPROBABILITY

Dawkins is fond of his "argument from improbability" and runs it as the "Ultimate Boeing 747 Gambit." He says that however complex any object X may be, a Designer of such an object has to be more complex and hence more "statistically improbable."

It's certainly true that *other things being equal,* the higher the information content of any object, the less likely it is to arise by chance. If you watch the operation of a machine that chooses digits at random, you are less likely to see 3141 than 31. On the other hand, randomness is a slippery concept: if you see 3141592653, you might well suspect that you were getting the digits of Pi and if they continued 58979323846, you would be pretty convinced. At one level, of course, a machine that calculates the digits of Pi is more "improbable" than one that produces random digits. However, in the light of overall background knowledge and other considerations, it may be highly rational to suppose that this is what we are dealing with. If we were getting the numbers from a computer, it would seem almost certain—if we were getting them from a conventional pack of cards, it would be very mysterious.

The problem of background assumptions is one reason that even with goodwill on both sides, the philosophical debates between atheism and theism can be so difficult. To most theists, it is utterly natural and reasonable that God exists, so to find a fine-tuned universe emerging from God's loving intentions is at least as likely as a computer generating the digits of Pi. Atheists view the world otherwise. These differences in background can not only change what people consider plausible but also how they evaluate the evidence.[30]

If Dawkins means to say, "However improbable a feature of the universe may seem, the existence of God is even more improbable *from my point of view*," it is impossible to gainsay this. He assumes God does not exist, so the probability is zero. But if he is to turn this into a cogent argument against theism, he needs to establish the premise that the existence of a Designer[31] is *always* less probable than the existence of a thing that has been (allegedly) designed. To show that this premise is untrue, a single, simple, counterexample will suffice. Consider an artist who makes a hundred drawings. There is a fire, and all but one are destroyed. Then the probability of the existence of a given drawing is 1 percent, but the probability of the existence of the artist is 100 percent. As so often in philosophy, it is much easier to see that something is false, than to know that it is true.

Appendix B
The Brain and Mind

For centuries philosophers and scientists have struggled with the relationships between consciousness and the body. We certainly don't think that we have solved the problems, but here we set out in more detail some of the ideas and arguments that underpin our responses on these topics, such as question 27 of chapter 4 and questions 39 and 40 of chapter 6.

We have described our position as dual-aspect monism allied to a belief in the poorly understood but genuinely causal properties of active information. There has been useful progress in both these areas in the last few years, and we think that we can give a somewhat less incomplete account than has been possible in the past. We make no apologies for admitting that our understanding of these issues is rudimentary—much damage is done to coherent thought by people pretending to more knowledge than they possess. The idea that nothing can happen unless its reason is scientifically understood is a pernicious falsehood. For example, superconductivity was discovered in 1917 and not scientifically explained until 1962. We still don't know what dark matter and dark energy consist of, although it is now appears that they comprise the majority of the matter in the universe.

In addition, it now seems completely clear that the brain is not a fully deterministic system. Thus the determinist ideas that have underpinned and lent a spurious plausibility to much of the reductionist agenda can be laid to rest.

MATTER AND INFORMATION

Consider the words you are reading on this page. There is a physical aspect: particles of ink are fused onto the page, and a chemical analysis could tell you a great deal of interest about the process. But it would tell you nothing about the meaning of the words. Equally, a complete change in meaning would make no difference to the chemical analysis,[1] and a change of the ink chemistry would make no difference to the information and the meaning of the words, provided that the physical changes still retained the ability to represent the information. Transferring the words to an LCD screen, a holographic projector, or even a hypothetical device that caused you to "see" them by directly stimulating the optic nerve would make no difference to the meaning. The information is logically distinct from any physical representation, but it is not a separate physical entity—rather it is an informational entity in its own right.

In these examples, there are some especially simple features that are contrived by human technology and not typical of the world in general. The first is that the book and the computer screen are carefully designed to display a wide variety of information content in much the same way. In general, to a far more obvious extent, the medium and the message are intertwined. But this does not mean that the informational content of, say, the *Mona Lisa* is not logically separable from its physical representation: just because something is less obvious doesn't make it less true.

We see pretty well everything in the universe as having a physical aspect and an informational aspect, neither of which is inherently more fundamental than the other—of course God has a mind but is not composed of matter, so *ultimately* the mental is more fundamental than the physical, but God is not *in* the universe. It is generally a category mistake if people confuse these aspects, and use informational terms to refer to the physical aspects or vice versa. We don't think that the physical and the mental are two different *substances* but that the mental is a part of the informational aspect of certain systems. The term we use to describe our position is *dual-aspect monism* to distinguish it from *dualism* and also from the now-popular idea that everything is physical—as well as from the idealism that was an equally dominant philosophical stance at the start of the nineteenth century and that held (roughly) that the fundamental entities were ideas.

These notions of physical and informational aspects are related to the concept of levels of explanation in ways that are too complex to discuss in detail here. Generally speaking, in any system of interest (such as, say, the heart or the brain) there will be a whole series of levels at which one can investigate what is going on. Each level (say, the cellular level) will have some "lower-level" components (such as the molecular biology) and some higher-level system in which it is embedded in some sense (such as the organ under study). Under the influence of a series of misleading metaphors, such as that of a deterministic machine, people have often supposed that the lower levels were more fundamental and that behavior at the higher levels was in some sense "explained away" by the lower-level systems. More perceptive thinkers have pointed out that even if the lower levels were deterministic, the behavior of the system is conditioned by the configuration of the components and there is downward causation in the form of feedback loops so that the system can only be understood in terms of the higher-level properties.[2] However, our view is that in almost all real cases the lower levels are never completely deterministic, and therefore the higher levels always have value in their own right.

Although we use the term *dual-aspect*, we don't take the view that there are *only* two aspects. Both the physical and the informational should be regarded as families of different aspects, perspectives, or dimensions. On the physical side we might, for example, be concerned with the chemistry of the inks and the medium on which they are written, but we could be concerned with the radioisotopes (if we were trying to date a scroll, say) or even with the physical characteristics if we were using the book to prop up the leg of an uneven table or to swat a fly. Similarly, words or other informational entities may have mental, artistic, or spiritual aspects: consider the phrase "*credo in unum deum*" when set to music by Bach and sung by an atheist—or Hamlet's "To be, or not to be" subjected to statistical analysis by a Baconian.

It's also worth remembering that the relationship between the informational entities and the physical entities that in some sense encode them is not simple. Although each letter may be located on a page, if you look closely at the letter you will see a collection of ink particles—or pixels on a screen. Any single one of these particles or pixels can be removed without changing the information—it is the whole set of particles, in context, that encodes the information in question. In the case of a hologram, each part of the information may be dispersed over the whole of the medium on which it is stored. And in some exotic scenarios for quantum encoding, information can be encoded in entangled states of particles that could be arbitrarily far apart.[3]

INFORMATIONAL ENTITIES ARE FIRST-CLASS CITIZENS

One implication of our dual-aspect monism is that informational entities exist to just the same extent as physical entities do: they can be considered "first-class objects" in our ontology and are not, in general, reducible to physical states.

We've already discussed words on a page. Let's look at other examples. Consider a piece of software like Firefox, the open-source Web browser. Where is it? It is installed in millions of computers worldwide. It is downloaded thousands of times a day. While it is being downloaded, each copy may pass through twenty or more computers. Master copies of the software are stored on a number of different servers, and within each server they may be striped across several physical disks, so that no single material failure can destroy the software. These disks will be backed up repeatedly. We're not, of course, suggesting that there is anything supernatural about computer software but merely pointing out that it is not "material" in any normal sense of the word. The only coherent language to use is to say that it has representations in, or on, material objects.

Now consider *Hamlet.* No original manuscript survives, and there are three distinct printed sources that differ in detail. Almost every performance uses a slightly different text: there are at least fourteen different editions, and performances are generally cut. It is absurd to identify any individual material object with the play itself. Furthermore, even if all the paper copies of *Hamlet* were destroyed, there are still innumerable copies on CDs, DVDs, and tape, and in cyberspace. It is possible that no original manuscript of *Hamlet* ever existed: individual scripts were prepared for each part.[4] It is even conceivable that these were lost and that the original printed copies (1603, 1604, and 1623) were based on reconstructions from the memories of various people. And, contrary to the delightful fantasy of *The Eyre Affair,* changing or destroying the original manuscript of a work does not change the work itself.

J. S. Bach's Mass in B Minor is a slightly different case in that the original manuscript does survive, although there are emendations thought to be by one of Bach's sons, so there are significant differences in the various printed editions.[5] Each performance is different, and there are hundreds of recordings and millions of copies of these. Again, it makes sense to say that various material objects are representations of the Mass in B Minor, but it makes no sense to say that it is itself a material object. It could be suggested that the Mass in B Minor is the set of all such material objects, rather in the way that mathematicians classically define the number 3 as "the set of all sets whose cardinality is 3." But there are a number of serious problems with this view:

for example, it would imply that the Mass in B Minor changed every time someone made a new copy of a CD of the Mass, or downloaded a performance, or erased or destroyed a copy. This, of course, is not a problem for mathematics because mathematical sets don't change. There is also no logical necessity for a piece of music to have any physical representation in order for it to exist. The Allegri *Miserere* was a "trade secret" of the choir of the Sistine Chapel, composed by Gregorio Allegri around 1638. In 1770 the fourteen-year-old Mozart heard it performed and wrote it out from memory, and it was first published by Charles Burney in London in 1771. As it happens, there were original manuscripts of this work, which are in the Vatican Library, although these don't show the embellishments with which it was actually performed. But there is no logical necessity for these manuscripts to exist. It is perfectly possible logically that Allegri taught his music to the choir, which then continued to sing it. The folk songs assiduously collected by composers such as Dvorak and Vaughan Williams are also examples of this point. Another example of an immaterial piece of music is Bach's Concerto for Violin and Oboe BWV 1060, which was a lost work and was reconstructed from his Concerto for Two Harpsichords (also BWV 1060).

Once we grant the point that works of music, art, and literature can exist without *being* "material" objects, it is logical to allow the existence of ideas; and indeed works of music, art, and literature can then be seen as instances of ideas. It also makes more sense to consider thoughts to be ideas rather than material objects. In addition to thoughts having many of the properties of music and literature that we discussed, this way of thinking about them allows for the possibility of two persons having the same thought or idea in different places, which is tricky for a material object—albeit not impossible in the quantum world.

It is logically difficult to deny that ideas really exist: after all the *idea* that ideas don't really exist is, at least on the face of it, self-refuting. Since our knowledge of matter and physics comes from our minds and thoughts, one would need overwhelming evidence to show that minds and thoughts don't really exist whereas physical objects and matter do.

This is not to say that all forms of physicalism are contradictory—such a strong result, alas, never occurs in philosophy. But reductive physicalists, who assert that only physical objects (whatever that means) actually exist, have to deny the real existence of many entities that are generally taken as existing, and the only remotely compelling reason that might be offered for accepting physicalism—namely, that "science has shown that all our thoughts are determined by physical laws"—can now be seen to be incorrect, as we discuss below.

We must now touch on a concept that we managed to avoid discussing in the body of the book: that is, supervenience. Physicalists have of course noticed that the idea that ideas, minds, and so forth do not exist at all is deeply implausible and counterintuitive. They therefore often assert instead that ideas and minds "supervene" on material objects. Formulating exactly what this means is problematic. The leading physicalist Jaegwon Kim finesses the issue by saying, "We will not need an elaborate statement of exactly what mind-body supervenience amounts to. It will suffice to understand it as the claim that what happens in our mental life is wholly dependent on, and determined by, what happens with our bodily processes."[6] From our perspective, Kim is stuck in a deterministic mental world that, as we discuss later, is simply obsolete and incorrect. It is also noteworthy that music doesn't make it into the index of his *Physicalism*. Murphy and Brown, in their *Did My Neurons Make Me Do It?* set forth a position that they describe, somewhat confusingly in our view, as "non-reductive Physicalism," in which they make heavy use of the concept of supervenience. Their preferred definition is "Property S supervenes on base property B if and only if x's instantiating S is *in virtue of* x's instantiating B *under circumstance* c."[7]

It is not entirely clear how this concept applies to things like ideas or music. The model might seem to be that there will be some physical subsystems that fully determine how the higher-level system behaves, what one might call "rigid" supervenience. For example, the laws of physics will determine how sound waves travel in a building, and therefore how the sounds from a musical instrument reach a listener's ear. But, as we shall see, the laws of physics do not completely determine how the musician plays, or how the listener responds to the music, or whether other concertgoers cough. Nor do they completely determine the behavior of the individual molecules in the air through which the sound is transmitted. Thus, in most real systems, supervenience, if it is to be a useful concept, has to be "flexible" rather than rigid: the behavior of the higher-order system is strongly influenced, but not completely determined by, the behavior of its lower-order components.

ACTIVE INFORMATION

So far we have mainly discussed types of information (words and music) that can be thought of as passive. *Hamlet* doesn't change, even though our interpretations of *Hamlet* do. It is therefore difficult, at first sight, to see how *Hamlet* can be said to cause anything—though obviously reading or seeing *Hamlet* can. It is, to first approximation, an object rather than an agent.

Software comes a lot closer to the kind of thing we have in mind when we talk of active information. Millions of lines of code cause our computers to behave in the ways that they do. Of course, most software seeks to be deterministic, and billions of dollars are spent carefully engineering computers and silicon to behave in a deterministic manner. But it is important to realize that determinism is not an *essential* feature of either software or hardware, and certainly not a necessary one. For example, in evolutionary dynamics we often use simulations in which randomness plays an essential role, both in mutations and in the selection of "partners" for mating or other purposes. As a matter of contingent fact, this randomness is generally introduced by a pseudo–random number generator. However, it would be quite possible to construct a computer in which random numbers were generated by physical processes that are known to be genuinely nondeterministic, such as radioactive decay. Furthermore, software can be self-modifying. One of the programming systems often used in evolutionary dynamics allows a program to construct other programs and then modify them, or indeed to modify itself. This is not, in general, good programming practice, and can lead to immensely obscure "bugs." But it is logically possible and is, in other contexts, an essential feature of problem-solving strategies: something similar happens when using genetic algorithms, where we use random mutations and combinations of possible solutions to solve difficult problems that are often intractable to conventional computational methods.

An essential feature of systems on which software can be run, so that the software can be said to cause events, is that the physical characteristics are such that many different outcomes are possible at the physical level, depending on the precise pattern of information involved. In many cases, there is no difference in the energy required to perform one operation rather than another.[8] Because of the careful and delicate engineering of a computer, the mechanism ensures that the specifically required operation gets performed. But this is a triumph of engineering, not an inherent feature of any system in which information becomes active.

Before digital computers became ubiquitous, analog computers were used to solve problems. These consisted of carefully arranged amplifiers and other specialized devices that were plugged together to perform specific computations, often involving complex differential equations. Analog systems inherently involve the possibilities of continuous change in continuous time. Suppose you are calculating the difference of two quantities, a and b. In a digital computer it is quite simple: either $a > b$ or $a < b$ or $a = b$. But in an analog system the concept of exact equality is highly elusive. For any conceivable mechanism that is meant to switch if (say) $a > b$ but not otherwise, there will be a range of possible values for a and b where the result will be uncertain. This applies even more strongly to a switching system that makes a decision based on some complicated function of thousands of inputs. Similar considerations apply to the timing of the arrival of the signals. Even if *a* and *b* are signals that can only take the values 1 and 0, if there is the possibility of a continuous variation in the time at which these signals change, then there will be a set of relative timings where the "decision" will be uncertain.

CLOCKS AND CLOUDS

Much of our thinking about the world has been misinformed by metaphors drawn from the world of machines.[9] However, as John has long pointed out, most of the real world is composed of systems that are cloudlike and inherently unpredictable, rather than clocklike. Nicholas spent many years as a computer scientist responsible for building machines that actually worked, so he knows from firsthand experience what we all know at least indirectly: making something reliable enough to be a machine is difficult. Companies like Intel spend billions on research and development and on advanced factories to make machines where a silicon wafer that is only 99.9999 percent pure is simply inadequate. A silicon wafer is unacceptable if the impurities are at a level exceeding 1 part in 10^{12} (1 in 10^{11} would be equivalent to one "impure" neuron in an entire human brain).

Consider a single nitrogen molecule in the air you are now breathing. On average it is travelling at about 450 m/s and bounces off about 7 billion other air molecules every second, thus 7,000 every microsecond. Suppose you knew the exact position and momentum of every one of these particles (even though this is impossible by Heisenberg's uncertainty principle), then perhaps you could, at least in principle, predict exactly where that nitrogen molecule would be one microsecond later. Of course there are all kinds of complications, such as electrostatic forces, angular momentum, and so on, but let's make it simple and pretend that these were all perfect spheres and that Newton's laws exactly applied—the kind of eighteenth-century worldview that shaped the Enlightenment and still influences much of our thinking. But suppose a tiny error is introduced in the angle at which this air molecule is travelling, for any reason at all. A little bit of uncertainty about the position of an electron, say. Call this error ε (epsilon). After one collision, the error is 2ε; after two collisions, 4ε; and so forth. Each microsecond this error will increase by a factor of $2^{7000,}$ or roughly 10^{2100}. The situation is clearly hopeless, even if the initial error corresponds to a Planck length (1.6×10^{-35}m—the smallest possible length, at which conventional physics breaks down) per meter, after just 97 collisions the uncertainty will be enough for the position of the molecule to be out by more than the diameter of a nitrogen molecule (6.2×10^{-10}m), which means it will miss the 98th target. This will happen in less than a 70th of a microsecond. And making the error one Planck length in the size of the observable universe (about 3×10^{23}m) just means it will miss the 176th molecule. So even with the unrealistic assumptions of a perfect Newtonian world elsewhere, exact determinism is dead. In fact, of course, we use statistical mechanics to describe the behavior of gases and liquids, and do not try to predict the behavior of individual small molecules. But many people think of the indeterminacy in statistical mechanics as simply a limitation on our knowledge rather than a reflection of real indeterminacy as in the quantum world. This kind of argument strongly suggests, to our satisfaction at least, that in cases like the movement of molecules in air the indeterminacy is real.[10]

Well, nothing much hangs on the position of a single nitrogen molecule in air. Why does this matter? Let's now consider a calcium (Ca^{2+}) ion in one of your neurons. It is about to dock onto a calcium receptor in a synaptotagmin molecule that will cause the release of a neurotransmitter that will cross a synapse and cause another neuron to fire. In order to get there it has to collide with a whole sequence of water molecules. The behavior of water is in fact complex, and there are significant quantum effects involved,[11] but even if we take the very simplistic view of water as billiard balls we can see a similar problem. Water is much denser than air, so in each second the calcium ion would "collide" with about 700 billion water molecules (actually it would have complex quantum-mechanical interactions with them which would be even more unpredictable). Thus the idea of being able to predict, even in principle, where an individual calcium ion will be is impossible. But we can calculate the statistical distributions of arrival times of these ions at any given location. Some simple calculations can give a reliable estimate of the order of magnitude, and it turns out that the mean time between arrival of calcium ions at these receptors is in the range 60–1,000 microseconds.[12] We will see later that this entirely destroys the idea that the brain is a fully deterministic system: there are of course many other situations in the brain where statistical mechanics works to give "random" noise, but this is enough.

IS THE BRAIN DETERMINISTIC?

If the brain were simply a machine where physical laws completely determined everything that happened, then it is hard to see how there could be genuine free will or real scope for mental explanations as opposed to merely physical ones. Of course, "hard to see" does not mean "impossible to imagine." Many philosophers argue for a "compatabilist" interpretation of free will that would allow free will to coexist with determinism—but we don't find these arguments compelling. It is perhaps easier to see how mental explanations could coexist with physical ones: we don't try to explain the behavior of software on a computer in terms of the hardware, let alone the actual gates and electrons, even though no one doubts that such an explanation could be given in principle. Fortunately there is now good scientific evidence that this is not the case.

The brain is a hypercomplex analog system in which about 10^{11} neurons are interconnected, so that the firing of one neuron will in general significantly influence the firing of others. These feedback mechanisms don't necessarily have to go through the brain. For example, you have alpha motor neurons that control the main (extrafusal) muscle fibers and gamma motor neurons that control the spindle. When a muscle is stretched, sensory neurons within the muscle spindle detect the degree of stretch and send a signal to the central nervous system, which then influences the alpha motor neurons. Thus in addition to the complex feedback loops within the brain, we have other feedback loops that "pass through" the body. Informational feedback loops may "pass through" many other systems outside the body as well—players of an online game may be getting hand-eye feedback from the other side of the world. This is one more reason that the simplistic "identification" of mind and brain is inadequate. Therefore, even if the firing of neurons was deterministic just 99.999999 percent of the time, given that neurons may typically fire 6–80 times per second, you would have thousands of nondeterministic firings per second. And because the firing of one neuron will influence the future firing of many others, detailed prediction of the brain state would be completely impossible.

One of the most basic functions in neurons is a comparator function, whereby a neuron will fire a signal if two other signals arrive at more or less the same time. This turns out to be influenced by many complex factors; indeed, a paper from Prof. Dimitri Rusakov's lab at UCL showed a significant influence of electric fields on the neurotransmitters in a typical neuron.[13] The typical neuron used in this study (the computer model for which was kindly supplied by Prof. Rusakov) will fire if the two signals arrive within about 10 ms of each other. But as the time between the signals moves towards the critical value (beyond which it will not fire), the delay in the neuron's firing increases substantially. Within 1 ms of the threshold the delay is more than doubled; within 0.1 ms the delay is increased by more than a factor of ten.[14]

Small uncertainties in the timing of arrival of signals, from whatever source, can be substantially amplified if they arrive close to the threshold. If a decision is very clear ("Run, there's a tiger"; "Ouch, this stone is hot"), then the neuron will get the necessary inputs well before the edge of the window, and

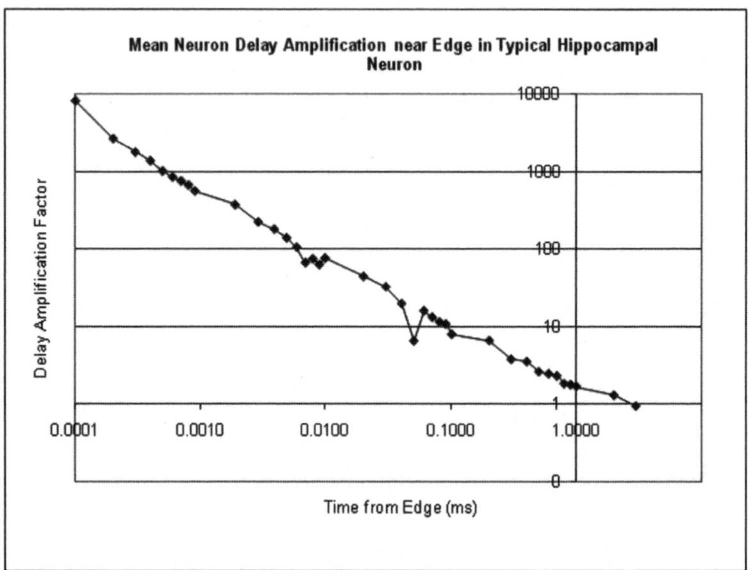

Delay graph adapted from Beale et al. (forthcoming).

indeed under these circumstances the uncertainties in timing are reduced, which is what we need to keep the brain fundamentally reliable. But suppose the decision is finely balanced: then the chance of the neuron getting the necessary signals within the time window is about 50:50, in which case the time between the last signal arriving and the edge of the window will be roughly inversely proportional to the number of inputs required. So if ten inputs were needed within 10 ms, the last input would arrive about 1 ms from the edge, and if a thousand inputs were needed, the last input would arrive about 10 μs from the edge. Neurons are typically connected to thousands of other neurons; in the human cerebral cortex 10–20,000 others is the norm. Consequently, if a decision is finely balanced, the chance of significant delay amplification is increased.[15] So an uncertainty of x in the timing of firing of one neuron can lead to an uncertainty of at least $2x$ (quite probably $10x$, and maybe $100x$ or $1000x$) in two or more dependent neurons: by the time this process has gone through k stages the uncertainty in timing can be between $2^k x$ and $100^k x$. Thus, by similar arguments to those in the previous section, it is possible for minute timing uncertainties to be amplified up to uncertainties of the order of a millisecond, which is definitely enough to make the difference between a neuron firing and not firing.[16] The uncertainties of the order of tens of microseconds that were previously discussed would take between one and seven stages, and going from picoseconds to milliseconds would take between five and thirty stages. This is, of course, by no means the only respect in which the brain exhibits nondeterministic behavior. At almost every stage in the process of getting a neuron to fire, there are stochastic processes at work. The diffusion and docking of neurotransmitters across the synapse is stochastic, and one important neurotransmitter (nitric oxide) is a gas. In the development of the brain it has long been accepted that there are genuinely stochastic processes at work, and it is now understood that brain development at a lower rate continues throughout adult life. An interesting survey of Indeterminacy in Brain and Behavior is given in a paper of that title by Paul W. Glimcher in *Annual Review of Psychiatry* 56(2005): 25–56.

So we begin to see a picture, although the science is in its early stage and developing quite rapidly, of how it is true that the brain obeys the laws of physics *and also* provides the flexibility to escape from physical determinism in precisely the circumstances—finely balanced decisions taken in regions with highly connected neurons—that are required to support our fundamental experience of true free will. At present the attitude of most neuroscientists to this seems to be that there are many sources of stochastic behavior in neurons (for example, the diffusion of many neurotransmitters over the synaptic gaps and the question of whether or not the sites at which they may dock are already occupied), but they suspect that ultimately these stochastic factors may be, at least in principle, deterministic. We think this perception is based on not having to think much about the interaction of quantum and statistical mechanics, and that many of these sources of stochasticity strengthen our argument that the brain is not, in fact, a wholly deterministic system.

It is worth noting that, in addition to the neurons, the brain contains about 10^{12} glial cells. Nicholas has long thought that these are unjustly neglected in accounts of brain behavior,[17] and there is clear evidence that they have significant roles in the overall state of the brain, being responsible for holding neurons in place, supplying them with nutrients and oxygen, insulating one neuron from another, and destroying pathogens and removing dead neurons. Even more directly, the glial cells called astrocytes clearly have functions that alter neural behavior,[18] and there is evidence of electrical synapses between neurons and astrocytes.

In addition, a couple of deep mathematical results support our positions. The Nobel Prize–winning physical chemist Ilya Prigogine showed that for systems of the complexity of the brain, even if their components were completely deterministic, there are solutions for dynamical equations of the system as a whole that are nondeterministic.[19] As the distinguished philosopher of science Jeremy Butterfield has pointed out,[20] the whole question of whether a given theory is deterministic or nondeterministic is far from simple, because if the theory is formulated mathematically in the way that is generally used by differential equations, the same theory can have *both* deterministic *and* nondeterministic solutions. We don't think people have fully understood the implications of this—after all, Gödel's theorem about the incompleteness of axiomatized arithmetic systems hasn't sunk in for most people yet.[21] Nicholas's collaborator Hava Siegelmann proved in the early 1990s that analog recurrent neural networks could have a computational power greater than that of Turing machines and must be considered as equivalent to "super-Turing machines," that is, Turing machines with an intrinsic true random number generator (see H. T. Siegelmann, "Computation Beyond the Turing Limit," *Science* 268 [April 1995]: 545–48).

It is also worth considering the evolutionary aspects of this. It is a fundamental principle of biology that if there is considerable evolutionary pressure for a trait and if it is possible for the trait to evolve in a population, then it will do so with high probability. If we take as a working scientific definition of free will something in the neighborhood of "an integral ability to take nondeterministic decisions when it is advantageous to do so" then there are clear evolutionary pressures for humans to have this characteristic. This is a fascinating emerging scientific field, but some preliminary thinking is as follows:

1. When the main evolutionary pressure comes from competition within your own species then you are likely to be playing evolutionary games where there is no single dominant best strategy: whatever you do your opponent can do the same and the result is likely to be a draw. Instead the games will be like Rock/Scissors/Paper—each strategy can win or lose depending on what the other player does. In such conditions there is a big advantage in being able to anticipate your opponent's strategy (if they play Rock, I'll play Paper). Once this ability is prevalent in a population, which requires high levels of social intelligence and is greatly facilitated by the use of language with names ("Fred always plays two rounds of Paper and then Rock"), then it is a great advantage to be able to be unpredictable and adopt a randomized strategy when it is in your interests to do so.
2. An element of unpredictability is essential to the development of new ideas. Just as random genetic mutation is essential to have interesting evolutionary dynamics at the biological level, so nondeterministic changes in culture and language are essential to linguistic and cultural evolution.
3. There is a large class of complex problems where stochastic algorithms (such as genetic algorithms or simulated annealing) substantially outperform deterministic algorithms. This would give creatures with an ability to add controlled amounts of randomness to their behavior significant advantages over fully deterministic creatures in situations where complex problem solving had survival advantages.

These factors and others would tend to give a selective advantage to partly nondeterministic brains. Similar results could be achieved by complex pseudo–random number generators, and presumably that is what people who believe in neurodeterminism assume is happening in the brain. But once we have freed ourselves from the mental shackles of presupposing determinism, it becomes clear that it is much easier in nature to make genuine randomness than a complex machine that mimics random behavior. In the words of a recent review in *Science*, "Nature knows how to make deterministic decisions, but, in contrast to Einstein's view of the universe, she also knows how to leave certain decisions to a roll of the dice when it is to her advantage."[22]

There are about 300 billion stars in our galaxy, but very few of them are in direct contact with each other. By contrast, on average each of the 100 billion neurons in your brain is in direct contact with about 10,000 others. Each connection differs in detail, and the exact biochemical and indeed quantum state of each neuron is different. Thus in principle there are about 100 billion to the power of 10,000 different possible ways in which *a single neuron* could be connected to the rest of the brain, and even if we assume that in practice only 0.01 percent of the other neurons are eligible for connection, the number of possible interconnections for a single neuron would be around 10^{7000}, and for the brain as a whole there would be a set of possible interconnections of about 10^{11} *to the power of* 10^{7000}. This is of course why the idea of genetic determinism of the brain is so absurd—there is not nearly enough information in the genome to specify such connections.[23] Another difference in terms of predictability between the brain and the galaxy is that the behavior of individual ions and electrical potentials in the brain matters. Since these are known to be subject to quantum uncertainties, it seems clear that the chaotic dynamics of the brain lead to an unpredictability that is not simply a function of our inability to measure precisely but an intrinsic feature of the system.

THE FALLACY OF MIND/BRAIN IDENTIFICATION

Although the indeterminacy of the brain undermines the only vaguely plausible arguments we know to suggest that the human mind is deterministic, there is a separate tendency to identify the mind and the brain. We think this tendency is deeply mistaken. From the perspective of dual-aspect monism, your body and your mind are different aspects of you. They are intimately connected, but neither can be reduced to the other. And of course there is far more to your body than your brain. To "identify" mind and brain as though they were synonymous seems to us to be wrong, and probably incoherent. First of all there are a great many parts of your body other than your brain that affect your mind: the eye and the endocrine glands, to give obvious examples. Second, it is entirely conceivable that a person could have mental events that do not correspond to brain events at all. Suppose, for example, that someone had an implant that extended his or her memory by means of an embedded computer (possibly located in a sinus) in such a way that the implant and the brain memory worked seamlessly together in the way that computer disks do. We take no position on whether this is in fact technically feasible, but it is certainly coherent to suppose that it may be. It would then be possible for someone's memories to change without any change in the brain. The fact that this is logically possible shows that the mind and the brain cannot be logically identical—however closely connected they may be.[24] We just don't know the relationship between the mind and the body: we don't even understand how general anesthetics work.[25]

LINKING BRAINS AND MORALITY

Of course, exactly how our minds relate to our brains and bodies is poorly understood, so it's too much to hope that conscience can be precisely understood. There are some suggestive

PET images about parts of the brain that are associated with moral inhibitions, which are clearly related to, though not identical with, conscience.[26] There is also an interesting paper[27] that suggests a correlation between people's genetic makeup and their willingness to behave altruistically. The Dictator Game is a simple game where you give one player (say) $10 and directions to share it however he or she likes with another player. Standard economic theory would suggest that the Dictator would always share it 10:0 to him- or herself. However, this is not what occurs in practice. Experiments with Dictator Games, and indeed with many other types of games, offer intriguing insights into altruistic behavior. The whole area of the evolution of altruism and cooperation is an exciting area of science, which is also attracting serious attention from theologians such as Sarah Coakley.[28]

WHAT HAS RANDOMNESS TO DO WITH FREE WILL?

For the reasons we discuss above, we consider it certain that the brain is unpredictable in its (exact) future behavior. However, unpredictability is not necessarily the same as causal openness. As the philosophers say, the former is epistemological (what you can or cannot know), while the latter is ontological (what is actually the case). What connection you should make between the two is a matter for metaphysical choice and decision. It cannot be settled by science alone. For example, there are two alternative interpretations of quantum physics. One sees its unpredictabilities as simply arising from a degree of necessary ignorance about the details of an intrinsically deterministic physics. The other interpretation sees the unpredictabilities as a sign of actual indeterminism. Both theories give the same experimental predictions, so the choice between them cannot be made on scientific grounds alone.

If you are a realist, as most scientists are, you will want to make the connection between epistemology and ontology as close as possible. That is to say, you will believe that what we can or cannot know is a reliable guide to what is actually the case. That is why almost all physicists take the indeterministic view of quantum theory. I think that our basic human experiences of choice and responsibility should encourage us to believe that the brain is something much more subtle and supple than a mechanical device of immense complexity.

Science's knowledge of the causal structure of the world is also patchy. For example, we do not fully understand how the subatomic quantum world relates to the apparently clear and reliable world of everyday physics. Chaos theory, which operates in the latter, is not reconcilable with quantum physics. The latter has a scale, set by Planck's constant, while chaotic dynamics is fractal in character and thus is scale free, the same all the way down. The two simply cannot be combined consistently. There is much more about these issues in chapter 2 of John's *Exploring Reality.*

People sometimes worry whether the unpredictability of the brain is simply another way of saying that free will is random—in which case is it really a free decision? This depends on what you mean by "random." From a physical point of view, all it can mean is that something cannot be predicted with certainty by the laws of physics. It does not imply that there are no rational principles behind it. An analysis of the text of *Hamlet* would show various statistical associations between the letters and the words, but it ultimately would have to conclude that the precise sequence of words was unpredictable. Thus, in a scientific sense, we can say that *Hamlet* is random, but there is clearly a deep rationality at work.

The scientific understanding of active information is still in very early stages. But it is now clear that we are not prisoners of our atoms, molecules, or genes. Our intuitions of freedom are real. How we use this awesome gift from God is central to the question of what it means to be human.

Appendix C
Evolution

The aim of this appendix is to describe in a bit more detail our view of how evolution and the Christian faith fit together, and to cover some of the more technical points underpinning our responses to questions in the main text that relate to evolution: specifically chapters 4 and 6. In order to make this appendix read in a coherent and self-contained manner, a fair amount of material from responses to questions is repeated here, so that people who wish to do so can jump to the appendix from any question. We beg the indulgence of any intrepid reader who has reached this point in strict sequence.

EVOLUTION AND THE BEGINNING

The Bible affirms that in the beginning God *created* the heavens and the earth (or as we would now put it, the entire universe) and that order, life, and humanity eventually came into being through his creative Word. It is not concerned with the scientific details of the process. The whole idea of "scientific," as we now understand the term, is a new concept: what we now call science was, in the early days, called natural philosophy, and the great eighteenth-century philosopher John Locke questioned whether natural philosophy could ever become a science. However, even if we try to impose this modern category on ancient texts, it is quite clear that Genesis is not trying to give a *precise* description of the details of what happened at creation.[1] There are two creation accounts in Genesis that differ in the details: Genesis 1 shows God creating birds, then land animals, and then humans; but Genesis 2 shows God creating humans, and then land animals and birds. The main reason these two sequences are in a different order is, presumably, that the main points of Genesis 1 and Genesis 2 are different. But it also makes clear, at the very beginning of the Bible, that we are *not* dealing with something that can be read in a simplistic manner. These are deep truths, not a cookbook.

One aspect of God's creating human beings "in his own image" is that we are given minds able to understand, at least in part, some of the scientific principles involved. The point in Gen. 2:19 that "whatever the man called every living creature, that was its name" also turns out to have some quite profound philosophical implications. Although the outside world is, to a large extent, a given, our perceptions and understanding of the outside world are strongly influenced by the decisions we make about classification and analysis, and by how we focus our gaze. Our ability to understand is shaped by our previous understanding.

Newton made a huge breakthough when he showed how you could account for the motion of the planets and many other material objects through a simple law of gravitation. Newton was a devout, though unorthodox, Christian although some atheist philosophers have tried to infer a mechanistic and atheistic worldview from Newton's scientific discoveries. The great French mathematician Laplace, when asked by Napoleon why he had left God out of his account of the universe, replied, "Sire, I have no need for that hypothesis." His equally great contemporary Lagrange, on hearing this, remarked, "Ah but it is a fine hypothesis, it explains so many things."[2] No one now seriously suggests that gravity undermines the Bible—indeed we see it as a wonderful insight into the faithful regularity of God that the universe is ruled by laws that we are able to discern.

Darwin and Mendel laid the foundations of a comparable breakthrough. Darwin developed the theory of natural selection, which gave a proper scientific basis to the ideas about evolution and the origin of species.[3] Although he was an immensely profound thinker and was fundamentally right about natural selection, he had hazy and mistaken ideas of the mechanisms of inheritance. Mendel, who was an Augustinian "monk" long before he became a scientist,[4] laid the foundation for modern genetics. Mendel was aware of Darwin's work but not vice versa, and no one realized the importance of putting these ideas together at the time. This held up the development of a proper theory of evolution for several decades, while Darwin and others went off on wild-goose chases after "gemmules." The delay may also have been in part because the main exponents of Darwinism in the Germanic world were virulently anticlerical and would have been reluctant to read great significance into the work of a priest.[5] Indeed, it was only when the necessary mathematics was developed by Fisher and others in the 1930s that it was understood how fundamental genetics was to evolution. And until the discovery of the structure of DNA, genes were in many respects purely theoretical entities. Curiously, we are now seeing that the picture of genes as simple sequences of DNA is far too simplistic, and genes are in a sense becoming more mathematical again. Indeed, they have many of the characteristics of active information that we discuss in appendix B.

At one level, evolution is a purely mathematical observation: given a population of any kind (animals, viruses, languages, or objects in a computer simulation) where there is replication, selection, and mutation, then (given a few technical assumptions) the equations of evolutionary dynamics will apply and will give insights, often very profound, into what is going on.[6] However, by the term *evolution* we primarily mean the remarkable scientific discovery that all known species appear to be related to one another in ways that can be described and analyzed by evolutionary processes. The fossil, morphological, and genetic evidence for this is now overwhelming.[7] In this respect, evolution is like gravity. Gravity influences everything in the universe—but is not the *whole* story of matter. Similarly, evolution influences everything in the biosphere, but it is not the whole story. And it is now clear that genetic evolution is not the whole story of evolution, with epigenetic[8] and cultural factors also being important.

None of this would have surprised Darwin. Exasperated by the overblown interpretations that others had given to his ideas, with absurd claims of universal Darwinism, he wrote in the sixth edition of *The Origin of Species*: "As my conclusions have lately been much misinterpreted . . . may I be permitted to remark that in the first edition of the work, and subsequently, I placed in a most conspicuous position . . . 'I am convinced that natural selection has been the main, but not the exclusive, means of modification'. This has been of no avail. Great is the power of steady misrepresentation."[9]

EVOLUTION AND RELIGIOUS BELIEF

A belief in evolution does not imply atheism. Darwin was also at pains to make this point, and many of the greatest scientists who developed the modern understanding of evolutionary processes, such as Mendel, Fisher, and Dobzhansky, were Christians, as are leading contemporary evolutionists like Simon Conway Morris and Martin Nowak. The idea that the religious establishment opposed Darwin is a complete fabrication. Many of Darwin's earliest supporters were prominent Christians, Charles Kingsley and Asa Gray (Darwin's first champion in America) being the best known. Leading critics of his theory such as Bishop Wilberforce made it clear that they were *not* criticizing his theories on religious grounds; indeed Darwin himself recognized that Wilberforce's published critique had telling points, and he worked on addressing them.[10] Far from being a pariah scorned by the religious establishment, Darwin was buried in Westminster Abbey, with the archbishops of Canterbury and York signing the petition that he should have this signal honor. It is certainly true that Thomas Huxley ("Darwin's Bulldog") had a quarrel with the religious establishment and was very much against Christianity, but he was also fighting about career structures for scientists in an era where much scientific work was done by clergy.

And just as the deep insights of Newton laid the foundations for the even deeper insights of Faraday, Maxwell, Einstein, and their successors, there is little doubt that the more we develop a detailed quantitative understanding of evolutionary dynamics, systems biology, and so forth, the more we will continue to discover unexpected new processes and phenomena. Indeed, one of the reasons that many leading physicists of the nineteenth century were opposed to Darwinism was that on the basis of what was then known of the physical forces of nature, they calculated that the sun could not be old enough to allow time for evolution to have occurred.[11] An important object lesson, therefore, is that when there is no known physical explanation for something or when something appears to be impossible according to the known laws of physics, it is by no means conclusive evidence that the thing in question does not occur.

It was only when Einstein's corrections to Newton's theory of gravity uncovered the possibility of massive energy release in nuclear transformations that the source of the sun's energy was understood. There may be natural tendencies in matter spontaneously to generate certain types of complex structure that are biologically accessible and functionally effective.[12] The history of life seems to have converged many times on certain types of solutions (see, e.g., Simon Conway Morris, *Life's Solution*). The religious believer will see these factors as signs of the inherent potentiality with which the Creator has endowed creation.

CHANCE AND NECESSITY

At the most fundamental level, evolution can be seen as the fruitful interplay between "chance" (that is, the contingent detail of what actually happens) and "necessity" (that is, the lawfully regular environment in which events occur). For evolution proper to take place, you also need notions of replication, mutation, and selection, but even in their absence fascinating developments can occur if such processes take place "at the edge of chaos" where order and openness interlace. If things are too orderly, they are too rigid for anything really new to emerge. If they are too haphazard, nothing that emerged could persist.

Consider the development of the stars. As we understand it, all the amazing structure of the universe—stars, galaxies, and clusters of galaxies—arose from initial fluctuations in the very early universe, just after the big bang. Stars are "born" from clouds of gas, die (as dwarf stars, neutron stars, or in supernovae), can be swallowed up, and indeed produce second-generation stars that are essential for life. Obviously this is not biological evolution, and the evolutionary processes that are normally studied involve many generations, whereas there are no known third-generation stars. Too little fluctuation, and there is no interesting matter; too much, and all is suffocated in disorder.

Adding replication, mutation, and selection to the mix gives evolution the amazing ability to generate new forms of life and organization. The following are rough definitions:[13] *Replication* is any process whereby new instances of a given type can be "born." *Selection* is a process whereby "fitter" types are more likely to survive in the population. And *mutation* is a process whereby new types are introduced. These ideas can be applied to many fields other than traditional evolutionary biology: for example, the emergence of cooperation in societies and the development of language.[14]

From a theological point of view, we can see necessity as the gift of that reliability to creation that reflects the Creator's steadfast faithfulness and chance as the loving gift of a free openness within which creatures can explore God-given potentiality in a process by which they are allowed to "make themselves." Such a world is surely a greater good than a ready-made world would have been.

MAKING A SECULAR RELIGION OUT OF EVOLUTION

Although Darwin resisted attempts by others to idolize his ideas and build them into an atheistic metaphysical system, some of his popularizers had no such inhibitions. Herbert Spencer coined the phrase "survival of the fittest" as part of an attempt to apply "Darwinian" ideas to social issues, noting that people who multiply beyond their means "take the high road to extinction . . . as we have recently seen exemplified in Ireland."[15] In Continental Europe Darwinism was also co-opted into an atheistic agenda: Ernst Haeckel, who made major contributions to biology and was one of the leading German evolutionary theorists, was also an aggressive proponent of *Darwinismus* who developed a "scientific" ideology of the German *Volk* that in the hands of others became the doctrine of the master race.[16] Attempts to make a secular religion out of evolution should be resisted: it is only the *scientific* aspects of evolutionary theory that should be embraced.

This is not to say that evolutionary thinking can shed no light on religious and ethical matters. One of the hottest topics in science is the evolution of "altruistic" and cooperative behavior. But biological explanations can only be illuminating and never ethically definitive. True altruism exceeds kin altruism (within the family gene pool) or reciprocal altruism (helping another in the expectation of return). When someone risks his or her life in order to save an unknown and unrelated child from a burning building, there is altruism of an order that exceeds evolutionary explanation. Darwinian thinking on its own is ethically inadequate, as Richard Dawkins acknowledges on the last page of *The Selfish Gene*. After 214 pages claiming that human beings are merely genetic survival machines, on the last page he says, "We, alone on earth, can rebel against the tyranny of the selfish replicators." Dawkins obviously (and rightly) thinks we should, but he has not learned that lesson from evolutionary biology. Although a great deal is now understood about the conditions under which "altruistic" behavior will evolve in populations, it is neither a substitute for ethics nor does it explain ethics away. It is interesting, for example, that the evolutionary dynamics of the superiority of forgiveness over revenge or even tit-for-tat is now quite well understood.[17] But this doesn't address the ethical or spiritual aspects at all, but merely the practical consequences, which, although relevant, are not decisive. After all, "take up your cross" is hardly an invitation to worldly success.

COMMON GENES AND EMERGENT BEHAVIOR

The sequencing of the human genome was an important milestone in science, but not quite in the way that was at first envisaged. Some of the most fervent proponents seemed to suggest that this was the "Book of Life" and that once the Human Genome Project was completed, "we will now cure diseases, weed out defective genes and create a new supergeneration in the near future."[18] Bets by experts on the number of genes[19] varied from 25,947 to more than 150,000. The correct number seems to be about 22,000, less than twice the number of genes in the fruit fly.

As Denis Noble explains clearly in *The Music of Life,* it is not the number of genes that counts but the way they are expressed and, in particular, the networks they form.[20] Adding an extra gene to a genome that contains 22,000 others can potentially make a huge difference. It is a fundamental property of complex systems that apparently small changes in the "static" structure can induce enormous changes in their dynamical behavior. Consider, for example, the behavior of the disarmingly simple-looking equation $x_{n+1} = r x_n(1\text{-}x_n)$, where r is some constant: this equation is known as the logistic map. If r is a number between 0 and 2, it gives rather uninteresting behavior, but it gets very interesting as r approaches 4. Even then, if we start with ½ we get the sequence 1, 0, and we stay at 0 indefinitely—"dead."

But if we add just 1/20,000th and start with 0.50005, we get a fascinating series of apparently unpredictable oscillations—which look very much "alive."

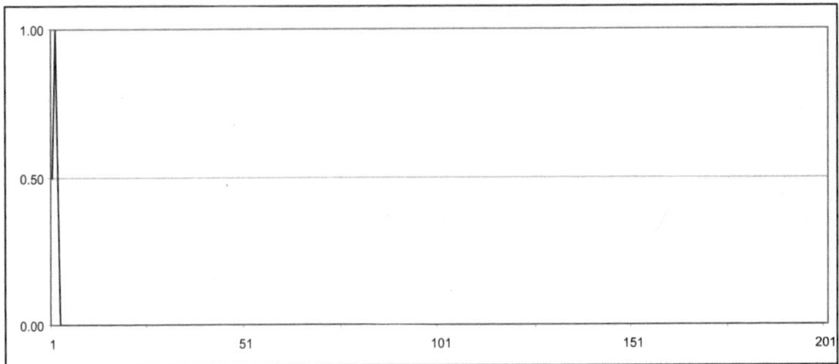

Figure 1 $x_{n+1} = 4x_n(1 - x_n)$ for $x_1 = 0.5$

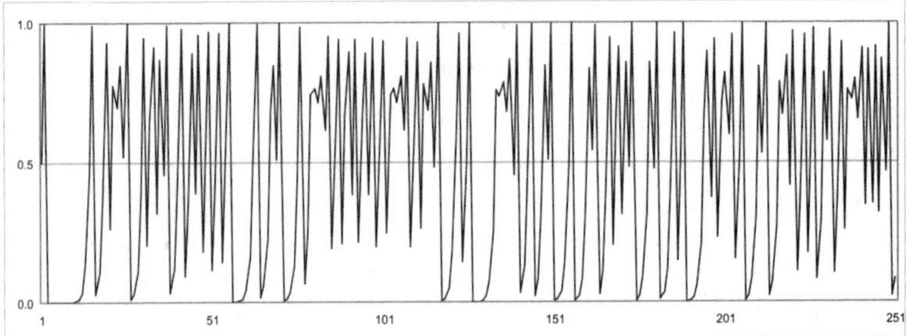

Figure 2 $x_{n+1} = 4x_n(1 - x_n)$ for $x_1 = 0.50005$

In any sufficiently complex system there are subtle thresholds that radically transform the system's behavior when they are crossed. If a system this simple can yield such rich dynamics, the changes that can occur in complex, or hypercomplex, systems are almost unimaginable, and we are in the very early stages of exploring them. Although we don't understand the details, it is clear that several of these thresholds have been crossed in human development: in particular the ability to use very rich and complex languages and, perhaps related to this, the ability to make deep moral and spiritual judgments.

The moment complex symbolic communication and language become major factors in the ability of individuals in a species to survive and reproduce, evolution takes on additional dimensions and can no longer be considered at a purely biological level.[21]

FIRST INSTANCES OF EMERGENT PROPERTIES

When the mathematics of a complex system is known, then it becomes possible to investigate precisely when new properties appear. In the case of the logistic map these are well known: for example, when r is between 3 and $1 + \sqrt{6}$, x will oscillate between two values forever, and "chaotic" behavior begins to emerge when r is approximately 3.57. The diagram below shows the possible long-term "equilibrium" values of x corresponding to various values of r, from which it is clear that the same equation gives very simple behavior for low values of r and enormously complex behavior as r approaches 4.

We are nowhere near being able to make precise statements about when intelligence or spiritual awareness begin to emerge, but for any definite property (such as "being over six feet tall," or "being aware of God's commands and capable of consciously disobeying them"[22]) that some human beings now have, or have had at some time in the past, there must have been a set of human beings who first had this property.

It seems entirely reasonable to suppose that the first set of human beings who were aware of God's commands and capable of consciously disobeying them contained both males and females, and that is what "Adam" and "Eve" refer to—as usual the Bible is far more elegant that modern terminology. Of course, when the Bible refers to forming Adam and Eve from the dust of the ground and from Adam's flesh, it is not trying to give "scientific details" but to state deep spiritual truths. All human beings are ultimately formed from dust, in a physical sense, and all are also formed from human flesh.

Some of our modern ethical dilemmas, like the question of whether it is permissible to do experiments on very early human embryos, hinge at least in part on when a property has either emerged or is on an inevitable path towards emergence. It is

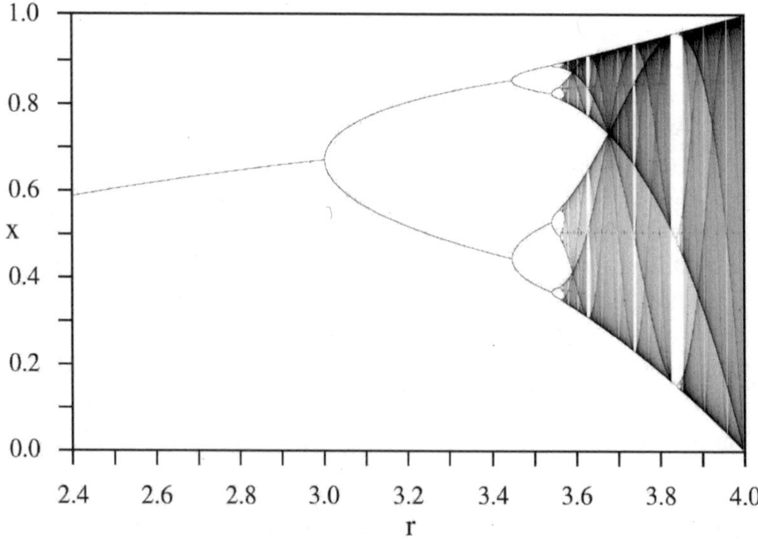

Figure 3 Possible long-term values of x in $x_{n+1} = r\,x_n(1 - x_n)$*

*Picture under Creative Commons License from Wikipedia.

important to be realistic about our levels of ignorance: a proper understanding of emergence in any system requires a detailed knowledge of the mathematics, and in most biological cases we are nowhere near this understanding, although great progress has been made in, for example, systems biology. But the fundamental point is that even in apparently simple systems, changes that look tiny can have dramatic results. This is true to an even greater extent in the hypercomplex systems of our bodies.

GENETIC DETERMINISM AND REDUCTIONISM

Genes clearly influence your biology hugely, but "genetic determinism"—in the sense that your genes inevitably determine your actions—is a nonsense that is not held by any serious scientist. Genes only act statistically—so they certainly *influence the probabilities* of certain outcomes, but they almost never "program" you in a wholly deterministic sense. It is not even true that two people who have the same genome would always react the same if they were exposed to an identical environment. Identical twins, who do have essentially the same genome, may look very similar to outsiders, and indeed the probability that they will have any given property tends to be strongly correlated. But even if hypothetically two genetically identical humans were exposed from conception to *identical* stimuli from their environment, the indeterminacy of brain outcomes would mean that they would not react identically in all circumstances—and of course it's not possible, in practice or even in theory, to expose two individuals to identical environmental stimuli. Indeed, it is now well accepted that there are many biological and developmental processes that are stochastic.[23]

As we have said, evolution is like gravity—it's a pervasive organizing principle but not the whole story. The same is true, to an ever greater extent, about genes. They are very important but by no means the whole story.[24]

Biological functionality is multilevel, and it is simply nonsensical to seek to reduce it all to genes. Genes do nothing on their own, and at every level in biology there are feedback loops between "higher" and "lower" levels so that the behavior of the system as a whole cannot be reduced to any of the levels.[25]

In addition, the fact that human intervention can change genetic makeup is now very salient. Darwin, of course, was very conscious of the power of artificial selection and carefully examined the breeding of particular varieties of birds and plants when he developed his theories.

So while we would hesitate to disagree with a scientist as eminent as E. O. Wilson, he was clearly mistaken when he wrote that "no species, ours included, possesses a purpose beyond the imperatives created by its own genetic history."[26] Species do not exist in isolation, and their evolution takes place in a highly complex web of ecosystems; in particular, the evolution of many species, ours certainly included, has been heavily influenced by human purposes. Humankind has long intervened in evolution, originally by selective breeding and more recently by genetic engineering, in order to provide animals and plants for specific human purposes. It might be objected that these crops or animals are only cultivated or produced because of their biological effects. However, this depends on the demonstrably false assumption that all properties of animals and plants are biological. Foods, for example, have a very substantial cultural and symbolic significance: the reason that some cultures will not eat specific animals, such as pigs, dogs, rats, or horses—whose meat is from a nutritional point of view pretty much identical—is not because of the "imperatives created by their own genetic history" or their "own biological nature."[27] The treatment of various animals in other ways is strongly influenced by nonbiological factors. For example, as Mary Midgley drily notes, "Pigs made the mistake . . . of being the sacred animal of Baal, which . . . has done them a lot of harm ever since . . . like rats, they are [a] glaring case of an animal that is treated without consideration because it is thought of as an embodied vice—an attitude which, whatever else may be said of it, is certainly not scientific."[28] Other examples of factors highly relevant to the survival, development, and "purpose" of a species that are plainly not "biological" are the use of particular flowers in certain cultures: roses as tokens of love, carnations for weddings, lilies for death.

Cultural factors are also highly significant in recent human evolution. The role of sexual selection—often downplayed by male evolutionists, although recognized by Charles and Erasmus Darwin—is important here. Cultural views of what is attractive change considerably, and there are good reasons to believe that power (essentially a cultural construct in human society) and wealth (entirely so) are significant influences on mating and child-rearing behavior in both men and women. Cultural factors significantly influence both conception rates and infant mortality, which are fundamental elements of evolutionary pressure. In Western societies the mass use of abortion also exerts significant evolutionary pressure: in England and Wales 194,000 abortions were carried out in 2006—29 percent of the number of live births (667,000). The total fertility rate in England and Wales was 1.86, and a 29 percent increase would raise it to 2.4: a fundamental change in population dynamics. It is also possible that cultural factors may have played a part in the extinction of the Neanderthals, which was one of the more notable events in hominid evolution.

EVOLUTIONARY BENEFITS OF RELIGION

The issues of fertility are discussed at a popular level in Eric Kaufmann's article in *Prospect.*[29] Women who had no religion at age sixteen are likely to have 0.44 fewer children (on average!) than the U.S. norm, whereas those who were Catholic or fundamentalist Protestant had increased rates of 0.13 and 0.19, respectively.[30] The fact that the average rate quoted in that survey is 2.05 suggests that over two generations, other things being equal (which of course they are not), the population of atheists has declined by over 50 percent compared to that of fundamentalist Protestants.

In the Pew U.S. Religious Landscape Survey (2008), people classified as "unaffiliated to any religion" are more likely to have no children living at home and less likely to have three or more children than the U.S. average. If we allow for the age distribution (unaffiliated have more in the range 18–29 years, the same in the 30–49 year range, but many fewer who are 65+), it seems that the average number of children living at home per Christian in the age range 20–55 is 1.22 compared to 0.94 for those unaffiliated—a 29 percent increase. However, if Christian families are more stable, this may account for some of the difference.

From a Christian point of view this is not an argument for the validity of Christian belief per se, but it does raise questions over the adequacy of a worldview that claims to see evolutionary success as the sole driving force of humanity and yet is demonstrably less evolutionary successful than people who espouse the contrary.

The statistical evidence for the influence in the United States and the United Kingdom of religious belief and practice (mainly Christian and Jewish) on health and well-being is overwhelming. For example, Harold G. Koenig and Harvey J. Cohen, in *The Link between Religion and Health: Psychoneuroimmunology and the Faith Factor*, summarized and assessed the results of one hundred evidence-based studies that systematically examined the relationship between religion and human well-being as follows:

- Seventy-nine reported at least one positive correlation between religious involvement and well-being.
- Thirteen found no meaningful association between religion and well-being.
- Seven found mixed or complex associations between religion and well-being.
- One found a negative association between religion and well-being.

Myers (2006)[31] cites Strawbridge et al. (1997, 1999) as showing that weekly religious attendance among a sample of 5,286 Californians was statistically associated with a reduced risk of death in any given year comparable to that of not smoking or regular exercise (a 22 percent reduction for men and a 46 percent reduction for women).

EVOLUTION AND COOPERATION

To a twenty-first-century scientist, the idea that love should be at the center of the deepest understanding of the universe is perhaps not as surprising as it would be to someone with an earlier scientific worldview. It is increasingly clear that almost nothing of scientific interest really consists of isolated pieces, each "selfishly" acting without regard for the others. Even "elementary" particles turn out to be collaborations of quarks, which never appear alone but always in pairs or triplets. Chemistry arises because particles cluster together in atoms and atoms join together in molecules, bound together by sharing electrons.

Genes are not particles that fight selfishly for their own interests—it makes no more sense to speak of genes being selfish than of electrons being altruistic—but patterns of information whose significance only emerges from the way in which they interact with hundreds or thousands of other entities within cells and organism. Biology is about organisms, not just genes, cells, or molecules,[32] and at the heart of multicellular organisms is an extraordinary degree of cooperation, in which up to about 10^{13} cells interact and cooperate in an immense variety of ways to produce behaviors and systems that are simply impossible for cells or genes on their own. Organisms depend for their existence on ecosystems embedded in the biosphere, both of which are examples of large-scale cooperative behavior between millions of species over long periods of time. It is an awesome thought that the atmosphere on which we and all known animals depend was originally produced by single-celled bacteria patiently working for about two billion years to remove the methane that appears to have been a main constituent of Earth's early atmosphere and to turn enough of the carbon dioxide into oxygen[33]—and that this atmosphere is sustained by a complex and potentially fragile ecosystem. The theme of cooperation runs so deep in biology and evolution that Martin Nowak has suggested that cooperation should be seen as one of the basic principles of evolution, alongside replication, mutation, and selection.[34]

We must not be misled by false perspectives. The universe is enormous, and from a physical point of view the biosphere, where life exists, is a tiny fraction, almost infinitesimal. But from the point of view of biology, it is the area of interest, and the vastness of the rest of the universe is almost completely irrelevant.[35] Similarly, the vast majority of living creatures on the earth are unicellular organisms, but when cells cooperate, a whole vista of amazing new phenomena, including animals and humans, can emerge. Humans, uniquely, can cooperate over immense distances, and new levels of behavior and understanding can emerge. Cooperation lies at the heart of most phenomena of interest—certainly including science. So perhaps when Christians affirm that cooperation, in its highest form of unselfish love, lies at the heart of the universe itself, this is another respect in which science and theology can find an unexpected kinship.[36]

Notes

Chapter 1: Leading Questions

1. See specifically Richard Bauckham, *Jesus and the Eyewitnesses* (Grand Rapids: Eerdmans, 2006); James D. G. Dunn, *A New Perspective on Jesus* (London: SPCK, 2005); Larry W. Hurtado, *Lord Jesus Christ* (Grand Rapids: Eerdmans, 2003); E. P. Sanders, *The Historical Figure of Jesus* (London: Allen Lane, 1993); N. T. Wright, *The Resurrection of the Son of God* (London: SPCK, 2003).

Chapter 3: The Universe

1. A current discussion of fine-tuning from a scientifically informed theological perspective is given in Alister McGrath's *A Fine-Tuned Universe.*

Appendix A

1. However, when he was writing, the evidence for a nonzero value of Λ was strong but not quite overwhelming—it is now considered almost certain. Careful analysis of the spectra of distant stars is consistent with a small nonzero value of Λ although there are recent suggestions that it is *possible* that these observations might be distorted by interstellar graphite. See, e.g., Fries and Steele, "Graphite Whiskers in CV3 Meteorites," *Science* 320 (4 April 2008): 91–93.

2. Even in the standard model there are a great many more apparently free parameters, and so far all attempts to provide explanations of the standard model have ended up requiring a vast number of additional free parameters.

3. According to a conversation with George Gamow—referenced in Martin Rees's *Just Six Numbers* (Oxford: Oxford University Press, 1999), 96.

4. We'd recommend Martin Rees's *Just Six Numbers* and Rodney Holder's *God, the Multiverse, and Everything* (Ashgate, 2004). The classic

book on the subject is Barrow and Tipler's *The Anthropic Cosmological Principle* (Oxford: Oxford University Press, 1988). Holder quotes Paul Davies and Brandon Carter as estimating that a change in *N* by as little as 1 part in 10^{40} would have this effect (Holder 2004, 35), though his subsequent analysis shows that really *N* needs to be about 10^{-39}. A detailed discussion is in Bernard Carr's *Universe or Multiverse?*—see especially chapter 5.

5. See, e.g., Holder, *God, the Multiverse and Everything*, 35.

6. This doesn't stop people from trying of course. See, e.g., Pogosian and Vilenkin, *JCAP* 0701 (2007) 025, "Anthropic predictions for vacuum energy and neutrino masses in the light of WMAP-3," arXiv:astro-ph/0611573v2.

7. Hawking and Hertog, "Populating the Landscape: A Top Down Approach" (10 Feb 2006) hep-th/0602091. See also Don Page's 2008 paper "Typicality Derived" (arXiv:0804.3592v1), which seeks to rescue quantum mechanics from the dismal conclusions of J. B. Hartle and M. Srednicki, *Phys. Rev. D* 75, 123523 (2007) [arXiv:0704.2630], such as "that much of cosmology would cease to be an observational science."

8. To give some flavor of this, and indeed the state of string theory in general, we quote from two recent papers: Baumann et al., "A Delicate Universe" (arXiv:0705.3837v1), say, "The attitude taken in most of the literature on the subject (cf. [3, 7]) is that because of the vast number and complexity of string vacua, in some nonzero fraction of them it should be the case that the different corrections to the inflation potential cancel to high precision, leaving a suitable inflationary model. This expectation or hope has never been rigorously justified (but see [8] for a promising proposal), and there is no guarantee that the correction terms can ever cancel: for example, it may be the case that the correction terms invariably have the same sign, so that no cancellation can occur." Krause and Pajer (2008), in "Chasing Brane Inflation in String Theory," say, "One of the key steps to obtain a viable inflation scenario in string theory is to fix all massless moduli, except for the inflaton," but "for a large class of D7-brane embeddings . . . cancelations are possible only for very small intervals of φ around an inflection point but not globally."

9. *The God Delusion,* 145–46

10. Ibid., 147. He also gives a simplified version of this objection on 143. "I see no alternative but to dismiss it"—more than one commentator has drawn attention to Dawkins's use of "argument from incredulity."

11. For a discussion of some of these ideas see Don Page's 2008 paper "Does God So Love The Multiverse?" (arXiv:0801.0246v5).

12. Hawking and Hertog, "Populating the Landscape," citing seven papers from 2002–2005.

13. In finalizing this section, Nicholas has benefited greatly from discussion with Lee both by e-mail and at breakfast, and from input from Martin Rees and Joe Silk, who are also highly sceptical of CNS. The result reflects Nicholas's position and is not intended to represent a consensus—but we are pretty confident that the differences between Nicholas and Lee's positions are not due to fundamental misunderstandings. Lee's ideas are continuing to develop and we look forward to an interesting dialogue.

14. L. Susskind, "Cosmic Natural Selection," arXiv.org/hep-th/0407266v1. He raises a number of other technical objections, based on current string theory. Since we (and Lee) are decidedly skeptical about string theory *as physics*, these objections may not be insuperable, but they do emphasize the point that CNS goes against both the standard model and current string-theoretical ideas. Note also that the evidence, such as it is, for inflation in the past does not provide strong support for the more extreme hypothesis of "eternal inflation."

15. See, e.g., the chapters by Linde, Tegmark, and Ellis in *Universe or Multiverse?*

16. For example: Black holes have enormous entropy and a singularity has little or none (see Penrose, *The Road To Reality* for a discussion of these issues). In addition black holes can evaporate and collide with each other, so what happens to the universes "inside" them when the black holes have ceased to exist? Lee points out that such collisions are relatively rare at least in our region of the parameter space—although decays by Hawking Radiation are not necessarily, and would be inevitable in a universe with infinite lifetime—so they would not much alter the statistics. But our main problem is that these events call into question, admittedly without formally refuting, the plausibility of the idea that black holes spawn other universes "inside" them.

17. Black holes come in several types but there is pretty good evidence for at least one "supermassive black hole" in the center of our galaxy and many others, as well as good evidence for smaller black holes whose masses are a few times the mass of the sun. Since there are thought to be about 10^{11} galaxies in the observable universe this can be considered a lower bound. There are also some deep puzzles about the entropy of black holes. For a summary of the physics see *The Road To Reality* esp. ch. 27. There is also a discussion of some entropy problems in Frampton et al., "What is the entropy of the Universe?" arxiv.org/abs/0801.1847v2.

18. See, e.g., Ashtekar et al., "Information is Not Lost in the Evaporation of 2-dimensional Black Holes," arXiv:0801.1811v2. Lee says it

does not affect the CNS scenario, that he has a lot to say on this and is currently working on it: Nicholas and Lee discussed a bit the weak and strong interpretations of black hole entropy.

19. Lee Smolin, 2008A, "Scientific alternatives to the anthropic principle" (arXiv:hep-th/0407213v3, July 24, 2008). See also Smolin, 2008B, "The status of cosmological natural selection" (arXiv:hep-th/0612185v3, July 24, 2008). Lee produces some ingenious suggestions for getting round the problems from inflation, but they don't seem very convincing to us.

20. See Joe Silk, "Holistic Cosmology," *Science* 277 (1997): 644, which contains several other criticisms of Smolin's theory stating that it "fails at almost every encounter with astronomical reality." Although this review is eleven years old Nicholas checked with Prof. Silk in August 2008 that these are still his views. In particular Joe does not accept Lee's contention that carbon and oxygen are required to maximize black hole production, and considers that hydrogen will do just as well. Lee points out that in current models of one-parameter slow roll inflation the 10 percent increase in primordial fluctuations would not occur (see Smolin 2008B).

21. See Smolin 2008B, 10-19.

22. You can (just) do evolutionary dynamics with infinite populations if you can assign a finite "measure" to each sub-population, but if the number of descendants increases infinitely in one time-step this breaks down. And assigning a specific "measure" on the space of universes gives severe difficulties with the infinite number of possible choices of the "measure" and the exploding free parameter principle.

23. After 100 years there would be about 10^{30} "mayflies" and 2 million "tortoises." Of course if tortoises had all their children in her first year they would outcompete the mayflies.

24. If the "generation number" is time then the "mayfly" problem goes away, but we have given reasons why it may be nonviable, and even if it could be made to work it is tantamount to making an arbitrary, albeit simple, choice for a timescale that in itself is a rather fine-tuned assumption.

25. At present some of the parameters of interest to Lee don't seem to have anthropic implications, but not enough is known about them to be certain. Keith Ward stands in a long theistic tradition of seeing God's choice to create this universe, rather than other possible universes, as based on a desire to maximize goodness (see, e.g., his *Why There Almost Certainly Is a God*) although of course this cannot simply be equated with maximizing some differential equations.

26. Smolin 2008B cites three specific predictions:

1. An upper mass limit of Neutron Stars of about $1.6M_{solar}$. So far this seems to be holding up, but it's difficult to detect and weigh Neutron Stars and impossible to do so exhaustively. Even if this limit proves to be correct, there are other conceivable explanations that don't require such profligate ontology or suffer from the other problems of CNS. For a discussion see Brown et al., "Kaon Condensation, Black Holes and Cosmological Natural Selection," arXiv:0802.2997v1.
2. Constraints on Inflation (if true). We're not sure that one speculative theory predicting constraints on another speculative theory (even if more widely accepted) is especially compelling.
3. Little early star formation. This is hardly a prediction since it is a well-established part of cosmology.

To the extent that these predictions demonstrate that CNS is a falsifiable theory they are a big improvement on many "string landscape" ideas. But they do not remotely constitute confirmation of CNS.

27. *The God Delusion,* 148. He then complains that God cannot have "a gazillion fingers."

28. Ibid., 149. Swinburne's excellent response to this and some other points where Dawkins disagrees with him is found at http://users.ox.ac.uk/~orie0087/pdf_files/Responses%20to%20Controversies/Response%20to%20Dawkins'%20The%20God%20Delusion.pdf.

29. Prof. Higgs was born in 1929 and attended the same school as Paul Dirac some twenty-seven years earlier.

30. To be a bit technical, in a Bayesian context, differences in background assumptions can alter the likelihoods that people assign, as well as the prior probabilities. In which case even deliberating on shared evidence will not necessarily cause people's conclusions to converge.

31. As noted in our answer to question 29 in chapter 4, we don't think Designer is a very good designation of God, but we'll let this pass for the present.

Appendix B

1. It might be objected that a change of meaning would at least change the exact position of the ink particles on the page, and thus have some consequences that are chemically detectable. But even this is not necessarily the case. The meaning of any set of words depends on the context, and in different contexts the same words can have completely different meanings: for example, "He's really wicked."

2. Denis Noble is particularly good on this, see both *The Music of Life* and his Ten Principles of Systems Biology (in Claude Bernard, the first systems biologist, and the future of physiology *Experimental Physiology* (2008) arXiv expphysiol.2007.038695v1) and it is also a viewpoint espoused by Murphy and Brown in *Did My Neurons Make Me Do It?* and the many authors cited by them in this context.

3. In addition to the fascinating emerging pictures from complexity theory there are related developments in evolutonary dynamics and even quantum computation. A recent article outlining the increasing emphasis on information in quantum theory, and pointing out that it dates back to the original work, is Seth Lloyd et al., "Quantum Information Matters," *Science* 319 (2008): 1209. DOI: 10.1126/science.1154732—although some of the hype around quantum computation in other popular writing needs to be taken with a large pinch of salt.

4. No one really knows, though I understand that it is considered probable that there would have been an original manuscript, although subsequent amendments could have been made only on the individual parts and not reflected in the hypothetical master copy. For the purposes of our argument it doesn't matter whether or not there was an original manuscript—our point is that the existence of *Hamlet* does not depend on there ever having been an original manuscript.

5. For example, the solo obligato in the *Benedictus* was assigned to the violin in all editions before the Neue Bach Ausgabe edition of 1955, when the editor, to general scholarly agreement, assigned it to the flute. Nevertheless a few conductors like Karl Richter and Herbert Von Karajan continued to assign the part to the violin.

6. Jaegwon Kim, *Physicalism, or Something Near Enough* (Princeton, NJ: Princeton University Press, 2005), 14.

7. Nancey Murphy and Warren S. Brown, *Did My Neurons Make Me Do It?* (Oxford: Oxford University Press, 2007), 206.

8. In simple computers this would be true for most of the operations, but with modern sophisticated architectures there are complex differences in the way many instructions are handled.

9. As Mary Midgley writes, "The heathen in his blindness bows down to wood and stone—steel and glass, plastic and rubber and silicon—of his own devising and sees them as the final truth." *The Myths We Live By* 1.

10. It can be shown that statistical mechanics arises naturally out of quantum mechanics, and is in a sense its limiting case. See, e.g., Huang et al., "Generalization of Classical Statistical Mechanics to Quantum

Mechanics and Stable Property of Condensed Matter," *Modern Physics Letters*, B18 (2004): 1367–77 arXiv:quant-ph/0506078v1. See also Rigol et al., "Thermalisation and its mechanism for generic isolated quantum systems," *Nature* 452 (17 April 2008): 854–56.

11. See Bukowski et al., "Predictions of the Properties of Water from First Principles," *Science* 315 (2 March 2007): 1249–52. They made a model of water that, with suitable approximations, could deal with 512 molecules for 30 ps. The fact that such a study was merited publication in *Science* indicates how very difficult it is.

12. For details of these calculations see Beale et al. (forthcoming).

13. Sylantyev et al., "Electric Fields Due to Synaptic Currents Sharpen Excitatory Transmission," *Science* 319 (28 March 2008): 1845–49.

14. Although the NEURON model is the standard used in neurological simulations, and is based on well-established physiological principles, it is impossible to say whether it accurately represents the behavior of neurons at time resolutions of less than a microsecond. There is, however, no reason to doubt its accuracy on timescales of 0.1–1 ms.

15. The brain is extremely complicated and detailed calculations are impossible, but robust order-of-magnitude estimates are (will be) given in Beale et al.

16. It has long been known that single neurons can have decisive influence on brain behavior. This is not only true in the obvious sense, but also, for example, Fujisawa et al., "Single Neurons Can Induce Phase Transitions of Cortical Recurrent Networks with Multiple Internal States," *Cerebral Cortex* 16 (May 2006): 639–54. For an overview of some of the complexities of the brain, and the limitations of the "Neuron Doctrine" see, e.g., Bullock et al., "The Neuron Doctrine, Redux," *Science* 310, no. 5749 (November 2005): 791–93. The detailed quantum behavior of Ca^{2+} ions binding to receptors will also introduce uncertainties at the pico-second scale. Normally it takes five Ca^{2+} ions to bind, but recent studies have shown that sometimes just two are significant (Sun et al., "A Dual-Ca2+-Sensor Model for Neurotransmitter Release in a Central Synapse," *Nature* 450 (29 November 2007): 676–82). In addition to these considerations, there are also electrical synapses in the brain, where cells approach within about 3.5 nm of each other and have junction gap channels of 1–2 nm to allow ions to pass through directly: these dimensions are also small enough for quantum effects to be significant. For a general discussion of the properties of electrical synapses (but not from a

quantum point of view) see Gibson et al., "Functional Properties of Electrical Synapses between Inhibitory Interneurons of Neocortical Layer 4," *J Neurophysiol.* 93 (2005):467–80.

17. They don't even get an index entry in books like Murphy and Brown's *Did My Neurons Make Me Do It, Consciousness Explained* or *How the Mind Works.* For some initial work on the interactions between neurons and glial cells, see Somjen et al., "Computer Simulations of Neuron-glia Interactions Mediated by Ion Flux," *J Comp Neurosci.* (March 2008).

18. See, e.g., Ishibash et al., "Astrocytes promote myelination in response to electrical impulses," *Neuron* 6 (2006): 823–32.

19. Prigogine's *The End of Certainty* gives a reasonably accessible account of this.

20. Quoted in Murphy and Brown, *Did My Neurons Make Me Do It?*

21. The great Oxford philosopher John Lucas published an argument in 1961 ("Minds, Machines and Gödel," *Philosophy* 36: 112–27) that human minds could not be completely deterministic machines because any deterministic machine is equivalent to a formal logical system, and any formal logical system *L* will, by Gödel's theorem, have propositions which are true, and which a human logician can see are true, but which are unprovable in *L*. He extended this argument in his 1970 book *The Freedom of the Will* and has been defending it ever since. Roger Penrose endorsed this position in *The Emperor's New Mind.* What seems clear, and can be called Lucas's theorem on free will, is that if there is a human being *H* who, given any formal logical system *L*, is capable in principle (with the aid of a sufficiently powerful abstract computer) of constructing a Gödel-type proposition *g* in *L* and acting on the basis that *g* is true, then no formal logical system could predict all *H*'s actions. However it is logically possible, although highly implausible, that there are no such humans, or that even if there were, other "lesser" humans might be deterministic. However, since there are in our view overwhelming arguments that the brain is not a deterministic system, and that the environment that might influence the brain cannot be specified by a finite set of discrete parameters, we think Lucas's theorem is unnecessary to our argument.

22. Richard Losick and Claude Desplan, "Stochasticity and Cell Fate," *Science* 320 (April 2008): 65–68. They are discussing the role of randomness in development: neither Beale et al. nor Liebermann et al. had been published then.

23. Of course it would be logically possible to specify an infinite number of connections if they all followed a prearranged pattern: the infinite number of digits in $\sqrt{2}$ can be specified very simply. But there is

clear evidence that the connections in the brain develop with true randomness—see, e.g., C. E. Finch and T. B. L. Kirkwood, *Chance, Development and Aging* (New York: Oxford University Press, 2000).

24. It might be objected that these implants could only act through the brain, and that therefore they were in some sense extramental. But it is perfectly conceivable that such implants could be linked directly to motor nerves, or indeed to other forms of input and output device. From our point of view, since the mind is active information, there is no reason why the physical systems on which a mind supervenes could not include some artificial parts, provided the essential hypercomplex, nondeterministic behavior is preserved.

25. Although significant progress has been made, this is still "the longstanding pharmacological enigma at the core of anaesthetic knowledge." See *ASA Newsletter* 70 (August 2006) and N. P. Franks, "Molecular Targets underlying General Anaesthesia,"*Br. J. Pharmacol.* 147, Supp.l 1 (2006): S72–81.

26. See, e.g., Julie Meaux and John J. Chelonis, "The Relationship between Behavioral Inhibition and Time Perception in Children," *Journal of Child and Adolescent Psychiatric Nursing* 18 (2005): 148–60; Joshua Greene and Jonathan Haidt, "How (and Where) Does Moral Judgment Work?" *Trends in Cognitive Science* 6 (2002): 517–23; Joshua Greene, et al., "The Neural Bases of Cognitive Conflict and Control in Moral Judgment," *Neuron* 44 (2004): 389–400; Mario F. Mendez, "What Frontotemporal Dementia Reveals about the Neurobiological Basis of Morality," *Medical Hypotheses* 67 (2006): 411–18; Carla L. Harenski and Stephan Hamann, "Neural Correlates of Regulating Negative Emotions Related to Moral Violations," *NeuroImage* 30 (2006): 313–24.

27. Called "Individual differences in allocation of funds in the Dictator Game associated with length of the Arginine Vasopressin 1a receptor (AVPR1a) RS3 Promoter-region and correlation between RS3 length and Hippocampal Mrna." (http://ideas.repec.org/p/huj/dispap/dp457.html)

28. Sarah Coakley and Martin Nowak, *Evolution, Games and God* (Harvard University Press, forthcoming)—the collected essays on evolution, cooperation, and theology from the "Theology of Cooperation" research project at Harvard, 2005–2008.

Appendix C

1. It needs to be emphasized for the modern reader that this is *not* a new position that Christians have taken defensively in the light of the

"march of science." Augustine of Hippo was clear about this in the early fifth century—see his remarks about astronomy in his treatise against Felix the Manichean (404), quoted in Christoph Schonborn's fascinating *Chance or Purpose? Creation, Evolution and a Rational Faith* (San Francisco: Ignatius Press, 2007), 55.

2. Quoted in A. De Morgan, *Budget of Paradoxes,* vol. 2, who claimed, "The following anecdote is well known in Paris, but has never been printed entire." The book was published posthumously in 1872 but was based on contributions De Morgan made to the *Athanaeum* magazine in the 1860s. Laplace published his *Celestial Mechanics* in four volumes between 1799 and 1805, so the exchange presumably happened in 1805. To be fair to Laplace, he may have been alluding specifically to the fact that Newton, in his *Principia*, suggested that God had to nudge the orbits of the planets to keep them stable. Laplace showed that the orbit of a single planet is inherently stable. But in a way Newton has the last word on this because it turns out that systems with more than three "bodies" (e.g., two planets and the sun) are inherently subject to chaotic dynamics and therefore unstable after all. This is particularly noticeable with comets and asteroids, and is a real problem for the continuance of life on Earth. Were it not for Jupiter and the moon (which is abnormally large compared to the earth, and seems to have been formed by a massive collision between a precursor of the earth and another planet), we would have been bombarded by many more large asteroids and intelligent life might never have had time to get going. See Ward and Brownlee's *Rare Earth* and also discussions such as R. Stone, "Near Earth Objects: Preparing for Doomsday," *Science* 319 (7 March 2008): 1326–29.

3. The concept of evolution was a commonplace of "radical" thinking at the time; indeed Charles Darwin's grandfather Erasmus formulated one of the first formal theories on evolution in *Zoonomia, or, The Laws of Organic Life* (1794–1796), as did Jean-Baptiste Lamarck in his *Philosophie Zoologique* (1809). Charles Darwin's fundamental insight therefore was natural selection and not "evolution" per se. A. R. Wallace had the idea independently, and they published simultaneously ("On the Tendency of Species to form Varieties; and on the Perpetuation of Varieties and Species by Natural Means of Selection" was a joint presentation of two papers, one by Wallace and one by Darwin to the Linnean Society of London on 1 July 1858). Charles Darwin's genius was not merely to have this idea but to work out the implications and lay out the evidence in such a scientific and systematic form.

4. The Augustinians are a religious order in the Roman Catholic Church—technically they are not monks but "Canons Regular," that is, ordained priests who also live in community and are bound under a Rule. Mendel joined the Abbey of St. Bruno when he was twenty-one, studied at the University of Vienna from 1851–1853 (aged 29–31) and conducted his seminal experiments between 1856 and 1863 (aged 33–40), publishing his results in 1866. He was elected abbot in 1868, and his scientific work largely ended. There were people who were aware of Mendel's work and Darwin's: for example, W. O. Focke's *Die Pflanzen-Mischlinge* (1881) makes mention of Mendel's claim to have found "constant numerical relationships" among the different phenotypes in what we now call the F2 generation, but no special note was taken by Focke of the "theoretical potential" of Mendel's work. Darwin had a copy of this book, but his German was weak and the pages mentioning Mendel were uncut in his copy—hence unread. The great Swiss botanist Nägeli had been a correspondent of Mendel's and knew of his work (Mendel sent him his 1866 paper) but didn't appear to appreciate its significance.

5. Similar religious prejudice delayed the acceptance of the "big bang" theory by some decades, which was also propounded by a Catholic priest. This is one of the few clear cases where a "conflict between science and religion" held up the development of science.

6. See, e.g., Martin Nowak's *Evolutionary Dynamics: Exploring the Equations of Life*.

7. This is well-summarized in Denis Alexander's *Creation or Evolution: Do We Have to Choose?*

8. *Epigenetic* basically means any hereditable characteristic that is not transmitted by the genome. See, e.g., Jalbonka and Lamb, *Evolution in Four Dimensions*, Denis Noble's *The Music of Life* and his "Mind Over Molecule: Activating Biological Demons," *Ann NY Acad Sci* 1123 (2008): xi–xix.

9. Quoted by Mary Midgley in *The Myths We Live By*, 62

10. Darwin wrote to his friend Hooker that Wilberforce's criticism of his theory (published in *The Quarterly Review*) was "uncommonly clever; it picks out with skill all the most conjectural parts, and brings forward well all the difficulties." Wilberforce had made it clear that he had "no sympathy with those who object to any facts or alleged facts in nature, or to any inference logically deduced from them, because they believe them to contradict what it appears to them is taught by Revelation. We think that all such objections savour of a timidity which is really inconsistent

with a firm and well-instructed faith." There is a careful discussion of the historical debate between Wilberforce and Huxley by the distinguished Oxford philosopher J. R. Lucas at http://users.ox.ac.uk/~jrlucas/legend.html. Wilberforce was critical of Darwin's views on pigeons and dogs, and Darwin's first work after the criticisms was *The Variation of Animals and Plants under Domestication,* which contains a chapter on dogs and two chapters on pigeons.

11. Lord Kelvin was the main protagonist of this.

12. See, e.g., Stuart Kauffman, *At Home in the Universe.*

13. The interested reader is referred to Nowak, *Evolutionary Dynamics,* for a proper discussion.

14. For a particularly elegant application see Liebermann et al., "Quantifying the Evolutionary Dynamics of Language," *Nature* 449 (11 October 2007): 713–16.

15. Quoted in Desmond and Moore, *Darwin*, 394–95.

16. As noted, Darwin did not endorse such extensions and tried to curb Haeckel's vigorous mixture of anticlericalism and science. However, it is futile to deny that the full title of the *Origin* (*The Origin of Species by Means of Natural Selection, or The Preservation of Favoured Races in the Struggle for Life*) is somewhat unfortunate with hindsight, or that Darwin shared many Victorian assumptions about "lower" societies. Discussion of "favoured races" was widespread and considered unproblematic in Victorian England—it being regarded as self-evident that the English were one of these!

17. See, e.g., Nowak, *Evolutionary Dynamics*, esp. ch. 5. From *this* point of view, Christ-like forgiveness ("always cooperate") loses out to a strategy called "win-stay, lose-shift." However, this is more a statement about the limitations of the method of inquiry (running computerized tournaments between players adopting different strategies) than a statement about deep ethical and spiritual reality. As Thomas Crean points out in his elegant and philosophically argued book *A Catholic Replies to Professor Dawkins*, a tendency, say to altruism, cannot fully explain a command "thou shalt/shalt not."

18. Tabitha M. Powledge, "Book of Life?" *Salon*, June 27, 2000. This article is in fact *disagreeing* with the proposition, but it is a reasonable summary of the hype that was going around at the time—*not* of course from the learned scientists who were actually doing the work.

19. Julia Karow, "Reading the Book of Life," *Scientific American,* February 12, 2001. See also the results of the Prediction Market at http://www.ornl.gov/sci/techresources/Human_Genome/faq/genenumber.shtml.

20. Although these networks are often called "gene networks," they are in fact gene-protein-lipid-cell networks (see Noble 2008), and it would be worth adding RNA to that list as well, since it is increasingly apparent that RNA plays a much more subtle and significant role than the traditional model of RNA as simply a mechanism for DNA transcription suggests. (See, e.g., Amaral et al., "The Eukaryotic Genome as an RNA Machine," *Science* 319 (2008): 1787–89—however, they persist in using the metaphors of "programming" and "control," which, as Noble points out, are misleading.)

21. This is nicely explored in Jalbonka and Lamb, *Evolution in Four Dimensions*. Nowak 2006 summarizes some of the work in evolutionary dynamics in cultural evolution—a rapidly expanding field.

22. It also requires that there was a time before which no human beings existed, which is pretty noncontroversial, at least in this Universe.

23. See Losick and Desplan, "Stochasticity and Cell Fate," *Science* 320 (April 2008): 65–68. They conclude, "Nature knows how to make deterministic decisions, but, in contrast to Einstein's view of the universe, she also knows how to leave certain decisions to a roll of the dice when it is to her advantage." We discuss some of this more in appendix B.

24. Noble's *The Music of Life* and Jalbonka and Lamb's *Evolution in Four Dimensions* both discuss some of the respects in which genes are only part of the story.

25. Denis Noble has now enunciated "Ten Principles of Systems Biology"; see, e.g., his excellent discussion in "Mind Over Molecule: Activating Biological Demons," *Ann NY Acad Sci* 1123 (2008): xi–xix.

26. E. O. Wilson, *Human Nature* (1978).

27. Ibid., 2-3.

28. Midgley, *The Myths We Live By*, 151.

29. Eric Kaufmann, "Breeding for God," *Prospect* (November 2006): 128.

30. Preston and Sten, "The Future of American Fertility." Ninth Annual Joint Conference of the Retirement Research Consortium "Challenges and Solutions for Retirement Security," August 9–10, 2007, Washington, D.C. http://www.mrrc.isr.umich.edu/news/events/docs/2007RRC/papers/B1p.pdf

31. "Religion and Human Flourishing," in *The Science of Subjective Well-Being* (New York: Guilford Press, 2006).

32. However, as Denis Noble points out in his "Fourth Principle: The Theory of Biological Relativity": "A fundamental property of systems involving multiple levels of feedback is that there is no privileged level of

causality. . . . Sydney Brenner wrote . . . that . . . the correct level of abstraction is the cell and not the genome" (Noble 2008, note 25), but the correct level of abstraction can only be defined in relation to the problem that you are considering, and in almost all cases there will be relevant effects from "lower" and "higher" levels as well.

33. This is a very simplified picture. The reality is, as usual, more complex and not very well understood. See Heinrich Holland, "The Oxygenation of the Atmosphere and Oceans," *Philos Trans R Soc Lond B Biol Sci.* 361 (2006): 903–15, for a more detailed picture.

34. Martin Nowak, "Five Rules for the Evolution of Cooperation," *Science* 314 (2006): 1560.

35. Not completely irrelevant of course, because for reasons discussed in questions 20 and 21 and in appendix A there are fundamental characteristics of the universe that are essential for life to exist anywhere.

36. John's book *Quantum Physics and Theology: An Un-expected Kinship* (2007) explores another aspect of the kinship of science and religion, which in our view is far more real and historically valid than the supposed conflicts.

Glossary

alpha motor neurons (α-MNs). Large, lower motor neurons of the brainstem and spinal cord. They innervate (i.e., provide nerves for) extrafusal muscle fibers of skeletal muscle and are directly responsible for initiating their contraction.

altruism. Selfless concern for the welfare of others.

anthropic principle, the. The principle according to which humans should take into account the constraints that human existence as observers imposes on the sort of universe that could be observed.

arginine vasopressin 1a receptor (AVPR1A). A protein that acts as receptor for arginine vasopressin, which is a hormone found in most mammals, including humans.

aseity. A theological term that refers to the characteristic of being underived.

automaton (pl. automata). A self-operating machine, or more specifically, an autonomous robot.

big bang, the. A cosmological model of the expanding universe according to which the universe originated from a singular point of infinite density.

black hole. A region of space in which the gravitational field is so powerful that nothing can escape after having fallen past the event horizon. It is called "black" hole because in classical physics even electromagnetic radiation (e.g., light) cannot escape.

chaos theory. A theory that describes the behavior of nonlinear dynamical systems that exhibit dynamics that are highly sensitive to initial conditions. In such systems, with chaotic dynamics, very small changes (such as a butterfly flapping its wings in Brazil) can in principle, under the right circumstances, have very large effects (like altering the course of a hurricane) some time later. This is commonly called "the butterfly effect."

compatibilism. The belief that free will and determinism are compatible ideas, in that it is possible to believe both without being logically inconsistent.

Copenhagen interpretation, the. The interpretation of the *measurement* process in quantum theory, espoused by Bohr and his colleagues, that assigns the reason for obtaining a particular result on a particular occasion to the effect of the intervention of classical measuring instruments.

cosmic inflation. The idea that the nascent universe passed through a phase of exponential expansion.

cosmological natural selection (CNS). A hypothesis (due to Lee Smolin) that the observed anthropic fine-tuning of the universe can be explained by a process somewhat analogous to natural selection, with universes having variable numbers of descendants.

critical realism. An epistemological view that claims the attainment of increasingly approximate knowledge of the nature of the physical world through a subtle and creative interaction between interpretation and experiment.

dark energy. A hypothesized form of energy that permeates all of space and tends to increase the rate of expansion of the universe. It appears to be associated with the lambda term in the Einstein equation.

dark matter. A hypothetical form of matter of unknown composition that does not emit or reflect enough electromagnetic radiation to be observed directly, but whose presence can be inferred from gravitational effects on visible matter.

deism. A philosophical position that derives the existence and nature of God from reason and personal experience, but rejects supernatural events and holds that God does not intervene with the affairs of human life and laws of nature.

Dirac equation. A relativistic, quantum-mechanical wave equation formulated by British physicist Paul Dirac in 1928. It provides a description of elementary spin-1/2 particles, such as electrons, consistent with both the principles of quantum mechanics and the theory of special relativity.

dual-aspect monism. A view according to which there is just one sort of world "stuff," one substance, which occurs in different forms of organization that give rise to the material and mental poles of our experience.

Einstein equations (or Einstein field equations). A set of equations in Einstein's theory of general relativity in which the fundamental force of gravitation is described as a curved space-time caused by matter and energy.

embryogenesis. The process by which the embryo is formed and develops.

embryonic stem cells. Stem cells (i.e., cells found in all multicellular organisms that retain the ability to renew themselves through mitotic cell division and can differentiate into a diverse range of specialized cell types) derived from the inner cell mass of an early-stage embryo known as a blastocyst.

emergence. In philosophy, systems theory, and the sciences, emergence refers to the way complex systems and patterns arise out of a multiplicity of relatively simple interactions. Emergent entities (properties or substances) "arise" out of more fundamental entities and yet are "novel" or "irreducible" with respect to them.

entropy. A measure of the statistical disorder of a system, central to thermodynamics and a key concept in many scientific disciplines, including cosmology, chemistry, statistical mechanics, and information theory

epigenetics. A term in biology that refers to heritable traits (over rounds of cell division and sometimes transgenerationally) that do not involve changes to the underlying DNA sequence.

epistemology. Theory of knowledge, a branch of philosophy concerned with the nature and scope of knowledge.

eschatology. A part of theology and philosophy concerned with the final events in the history of the world, or the ultimate destiny of creation.

Euthyphro dilemma, the: A dilemma found in Plato's dialogue *Euthyphro*, in which Socrates asks Euthyphro, "Is the pious loved by the gods because it is pious, or is it pious because it is loved by the gods?"

evolutionary psychology. A theoretical approach to psychology that attempts to explain mental and psychological traits such as memory, perception, or language as adaptations, that is, as the functional products of natural selection or sexual selection.

exploding free parameters postulate. The idea that any theory that seeks to explain the fine-tuning of the standard model eventually has more free parameters than are explained.

extrafusal muscle fibers. A class of muscle fiber innervated (i.e., connected to nerves) by alpha motor neurons.

falsifiability. The logical possibility that an assertion can be shown false by an observation or a physical experiment.

gamma motor neurons. A component of the fusimotor system, the system by which the central nervous system controls muscle spindle sensitivity.

general relativity (or general theory of relativity). The geometric theory of gravitation originated by Albert Einstein in 1915/16. It unifies special relativity, Newton's law of universal gravitation, and the insight that gravitation can be described by the curvature of space and time.

gemmules. Imagined particles of inheritance proposed by Darwin, which were assumed to be shed by the organs of the body and carried in the bloodstream to the reproductive organs, where they accumulated in the germ cells or gametes.

Generous Tit-for-Tat. A strategy in iterated Prisoners Dilemma whereby you Cooperate with a player who Cooperates or only occasionally Defects.

genetic circuit. A biological system in which the outputs from the biochemical behavior of one gene or set of genes are considered as the inputs to behavior of others, so that the behavior of the system can be considered and analyzed in ways somewhat analogous to an electrical circuit.

genetic determinism. The idea that genes determine, as opposed to influence, physical and behavioral phenotypes (i.e., any observed quality of an organism, such as its morphology, development, or behavior).

God of the gaps. The idea that anything that can be explained by human knowledge is not in the domain of God.

Gödel's incompleteness theorems. These theorems in mathematical logic establish inherent limitations of all but the most trivial formal systems for arithmetic of mathematical interest. Specifically, no formal system rich enough to contain elementary arithmetic can be both complete and consistent—that is, if such a system is consistent there will always be true propositions that cannot be proven within the system.

grand unified theory. A theory or model in physics that assumes that the electromagnetic, weak nuclear, and strong nuclear forces can all be unified and at sufficiently high energies become the same.

Heisenberg's uncertainty principle. The principle in quantum mechanics that you cannot simultaneously measure two aspects of a quantum object (such as position and momentum) with arbitrary precision.

Kalam cosmological argument. A version of the cosmological argument derived from the Islamic Kalam form of dialectical argument. It attempts to prove the existence of God by appealing to the principle of universal cause.

kenosis. A Greek word for emptiness. It is used both as a description of the incarnation and as an indication of the nature of God's activity and condescension. It is also used to refer to God's self-limitation.

logic gate. A logic gate performs a logical operation on one or more logic inputs and produces a single logic output.

logistic map. A polynomial mapping, often cited as an archetypal example of how complex, chaotic behavior can arise from simple, nonlinear dynamical equations.

loop quantum gravity. A proposed quantum theory of space-time distinct from string theory that attempts to reconcile the seemingly incompatible theories of quantum mechanics and general relativity.

measurement problem, the. Quantum theory in general predicts only the relative probabilities of a variety of different outcomes of each act of measurement. How an observer records a particular such outcome in any single act of measurement is an unresolved interpretative problem.

mechanism (mechanistic worldview). A philosophical worldview that combines physicalism with determinism.

microtubules. One of the components of the cytoskeleton (i.e., a cellular "scaffolding" or "skeleton" contained within the cytoplasm, which is a gelatinous, semitransparent fluid that fills most cells). They serve as structural components within cells and are involved in many cellular processes.

m-theory. The name given to various further conjectural extensions and generalizations of string theories.

multiverse. The hypothetical set of multiple universes (including our universe) that together supposedly comprise all physical reality. The different universes within the multiverse are sometimes called parallel universes.

Neanderthals. A species of the *Homo* genus (*Homo neanderthalensis*) that inhabited Europe and parts of western and central Asia: possibly a subspecies of *Homo sapiens* (*Homo sapiens neanderthalis*).

neural substrate. The set of brain structures that underlies a specific behavior or psychological state.

neutron star. A star formed from the collapsed remnant of a massive star.

Newtonian mechanics. The initial stage in the development of classical mechanics, which is used for describing the motion of macroscopic objects, from projectiles to parts of machinery as well as to astronomical objects, such as spacecraft, planets, stars, and galaxies.

ontology. The study of conceptions of reality and the nature of being. In philosophy, ontology is the study of being or existence and constitutes the basic subject matter of metaphysics.

orchestrated object reduction. A term coined by Roger Penrose and Stuart Hameroff to refer to their speculation that human consciousness is the result of quantum gravity effects in microtubules.

original sin. In Christian theology, original sin is humanity's state of sin, resulting from the fall of humans.

PET. Positron Emission Tomography (PET) is a medical imaging technique in which a small amount of radioactive tracer is given to the patient, normally by injecting it into a vein.

physicalism. The thesis that everything is physical or can be reduced to the physical.

Planck's constant. The ratio of the energy of a photon to its frequency.

Prisoners Dilemma. A game in which two players each decide to Defect or Cooperate, and it pays each player to Defect if the other Cooperates but if both Defect they are worse off than if both Cooperate. Iterated over many rounds, this is a fundamental evolutionary game.

qualia. Qualities or sensations, like redness or pain, considered independently of their effects on behavior and from whatever physical circumstances that give rise to them.

quantum computation. A process of computation that makes direct use of distinctively quantum-mechanical phenomena, such as superposition and entanglement, to perform operations on data.

quantum consciousness. The idea that quantum mechanics is intimately and directly linked to an explanation of consciousness.

quantum gravity. The field of theoretical physics attempting to unify quantum mechanics, which describes three of the fundamental forces of nature, with general relativity, the theory of the fourth fundamental force, gravity.

quantum theory. This term may mean (1) old quantum theory under the Bohr model; (2) quantum mechanics, an umbrella term sometimes for all of quantum physics, but sometimes for just nonrelativistic theories; (3) quantum field theory, a generic type of relativistic quantum theory, which includes quantum electrodynamics, quantum chromodynamics, or electroweak interaction; (4) quantum gravity, a general term for theories intended to quanticize general relativity; or (5) quantum optics.

quantum vacuum. In quantum field theory, this refers to the quantum state with the lowest possible energy, which generally contains no physical particles. However, the quantum vacuum is teeming with "virtual particles" that can exist for a short time due to the uncertainty principle and can have major effects.

randomness. A lack of order, purpose, cause, or predictability in nonscientific parlance. In statistics, a random process is a repeatable process whose outcomes follow no describable deterministic pattern, but follow a probability distribution.

reductionism. An approach to understanding the nature of complex things by reducing them to their parts. Philosophical reductionism refers to a position that a complex system can be understood entirely in terms of its parts. Methodological reductionism refers to a strategy for trying to understand things by understanding their constituents.

second law of thermodynamics, the. An expression of the universal law of increasing entropy, stating that the entropy of an isolated system that is not in equilibrium will tend to increase over time, approaching a maximum value at equilibrium.

serial big crunch model. The idea that the universe might have expanded, then contracted, and then expanded again, thus generating a potentially infinite number of universes.

string theory, the. An incomplete but popular approach to theoretical physics, whose building blocks were originally one-dimensional extended objects called strings, rather than the point particles that form the basis for the standard model of particle physics. It now generally assumes that space-time has ten or eleven dimensions, but many of them are rolled up to be invisible to us.

supernova. A stellar explosion that is extremely luminous and causes a burst of radiation that may briefly outshine an entire galaxy before fading from view over several weeks or months.

super-Turing machine. A mathematical model of a nondeterministic digital computer that is a Turing machine also equipped with a true random number generator.

theodicy. A specific branch of theology and philosophy that attempts to reconcile the existence of evil or suffering in the world with the belief in an omniscient, omnipotent, and benevolent God—that is, it is an attempt to solve the problem of evil.

theory of everything. A hypothetical theory of theoretical physics that would fully explain and link together all known physical phenomena. Now considered by former advocates such as Stephen Hawking to be impossible, due to Gödel's theorems.

Tit-for-Tat. A strategy in an evolutionary game such as iterated Prisoners Dilemma in which you Cooperate if the other player Cooperated and Defect if they Defected.

Turing machine. A mathematical model of a deterministic digital computer due to Alan Turing, involving a potentially infinite "tape" that has a finite number of symbols from a finite alphabet, and a finite set of rules for the machine reading and writing to the tape. The term also refers to any computational system that is mathematically equivalent to a Turing machine, and this includes essentially all extant digital computers.

univeralism. A theological thesis according to which all persons will be reconciled to God.

vacuum fluctuations (or virtual particles). Particles created and destroyed out of the quantum vacuum in particle-antiparticle pairs, which shortly annihilate each other and disappear.

verisimilitude. Likeness or resemblance of the truth, reality, or a fact's probability.

wave function. A mathematical tool used in quantum mechanics to describe any physical system. It is a complex-valued function defined over space and time, from which the probabilities of observing various properties of the object can be deduced.

Selected Bibliography

Alexander, Denis. 2008. *Creation and Evolution: Do We Have to Choose?* Oxford: Monarch.

Barrow, J. D., and F. J. Tipler. 1986. *The Anthropic Cosmological Principle*. Oxford: Oxford University Press.

Bauckham, Richard. 2006. *Jesus and the Eyewitnesses*. Grand Rapids: Eerdmans.

Burleigh, Michael. 2005. *Earthly Powers: The Clash of Religion and Politics in Europe, from the French Revolution to the Great War*. New York: HarperCollins.

———. 2007. *Sacred Causes: The Clash of Religion and Politics, from the Great War to the War on Terror*. New York: HarperCollins.

Carr, Bernard, ed. 2007. *Universe or Multiverse?* Cambridge: Cambridge University Press.

Coakley, Sarah, and Martin Nowak, eds. 2009. *Evolution, Games and God*. Cambridge: Harvard University Press.

Conway Morris, Simon. 2003. *Life's Solution: Inevitable Humans in a Lonely Universe*. Cambridge: Cambridge University Press.

Cornwell, John. 2007. *Darwin's Angel: An Angelic Riposte to the God Delusion*. London: Profile.

Cottingham, John. 2005. *The Spiritual Dimension*. Cambridge: Cambridge University Press.

Crean, Thomas. 2007. *A Catholic Replies to Professor Dawkins* [published in the U.S. as *God Is No Delusion: A Refutation of Richard Dawkins*]. San Francisco: Ignatius Press.

Darwin, Charles. *The Origin of Species by Means of Natural Selection; or, The Preservation of Favoured Races in the Struggle for Life*. New York: D. Appleton and Co., 1868.

Davies, Paul. 1992. *The Mind of God: The Scientific Basis for a Rational World*. New York: Touchstone.

Dawkins, Richard. 1978. *The Selfish Gene*. Oxford: Oxford University Press.

———. 2006. *The God Delusion*. New York: Mariner Books.
Dennett, Daniel. 1992. *Consciousness Explained*. Boston: Back Bay Books.
Desmond, Adrian, and John Moore. 1991. *Darwin*. London: Michael Joseph.
Dunn, James D. G. 2005. *A New Perspective on Jesus*. London: SPCK.
Forde, Jasper. 2002. *The Eyre Affair*. London: Penguin.
Gumbel, Nicky. 2008. *Is God a Delusion?* London: Alpha International.
Hefner, Philip. 2000. *The Human Factor: Evolution, Culture and Religion*. Theology and the Sciences. Minneapolis: Augsburg Fortress.
Hick, John. 1978. *Evil and the God of Love*. Rev. ed. San Francisco: Harper San Francisco.
Holder, Rodney. 2004. *God, the Multiverse, and Everything: Modern Cosmology and the Argument from Design*. Aldershot: Ashgate.
Hurtado, Larry W. *Lord Jesus Christ*. Grand Rapids: Eerdmans, 2003.
Jalbonka, Eva, and Mary Lamb. 2005. *Evolution in Four Dimensions: Genetic, Epigenetic, Behavioral, and Symbolic Variation in the History of Life*. Cambridge: MIT Press.
Kauffman, Stuart. 1995. *At Home in the Universe: The Search for the Laws of Self-Organization and Complexity*. Oxford: Oxford University Press.
Kim, Jaegwon. 2005. *Physicalism, or Something Near Enough*. Princeton, NJ: Princeton University Press.
Koenig, Harold G., and Harvey J. Cohen. 2001. *The Link between Religion and Health: Psychoneuroimmunology and the Faith Factor*. Oxford: Oxford University Press.
Lucas, John. 1970. *The Freedom of the Will*. Oxford: Oxford University Press.
McGrath, Alister. 2004. *Dawkins' God: Genes, Memes, and the Meaning of Life*. Oxford: Wiley-Blackwell.
———. 2004. *The Twilight of Atheism: The Rise and Fall of Disbelief in the Modern World*. New York: Doubleday.
———. 2007. *The Dawkins Delusion: Atheist Fundamentalism and the Denial of the Divine*. Oxford: IVP Books.
———. 2009. *A Fine-Tuned Universe: The Quest for God in Science and Theology*. Louisville, KY: Westminster John Knox Press.
Midgley, Mary. 2004. *The Myths We Live By*. Oxford: Routledge.
Murphy, Nancey, and Warren S. Brown. 2007. *Did My Neurons Make Me Do It? Philosophical and Neurobiological Perspectives on Moral Responsibility and Free Will*. Oxford: Oxford University Press.

Noble, Denis. 2006. *The Music of Life*. Oxford: Oxford University Press.

Peacocke, Arthur. 2004. *Creation and the World of Science*. Rev. ed. Oxford: Oxford University Press.

Penrose, Roger. 2002. *The Emperor's New Mind: Concerning Computers, Minds, and the Laws of Physics*. Oxford: Oxford University Press.

———. 2007. *The Road to Reality: A Complete Guide to the Laws of the Universe*. 2nd ed. New York: Vintage.

Pinker, Steven. 1999. *How the Mind Works*. Boston: Norton.

Plantinga, Alvin. 1977. *God, Freedom, and Evil.* Grand Rapids: Eerdmans.

———. 1990. *God and Other Minds: A Study of the Rational Justification of Belief in God.* Ithaca: Cornell University Press.

Polkinghorne, John. 1996. *The Faith of a Physicist: Reflections of a Bottom-Up Thinker.* Ausburg Fortress Press [published in the UK as *Science and Christian Belief*].

———. 1996. *Scientists as Theologians*. London: SPCK.

———. 1998. *Belief in God in an Age of Science*. New Haven: Yale University Press.

———. 2001. *Faith, Science and Understanding*. New Haven: Yale University Press.

———. 2003. *The God of Hope and the End of the World.* New Haven: Yale University Press.

———. 2005. *Exploring Reality: The Intertwining of Science and Religion*. London: SPCK.

———. 2005. *Science and Providence: God's Interaction with the World.* Templeton Foundation Press.

———. 2006. *Science and Creation: The Search for Understanding.* Philadelphia: Templeton Foundation Press.

———. 2007. *Exploring Reality: The Intertwining of Science and Religion*. New Haven: Yale University Press.

———. 2008. *Quantum Physics and Theology: An Unexpected Kinship*. New Haven: Yale University Press.

Polyani, Michael. 1962. *Personal Knowledge towards a Post-Critical Philosophy Knowledge*. New York: Harper & Row.

Prigogine, Ilya. 1997. *The End of Certainty*. New York: Free Press.

Ruse, Michael. 2000. *Can a Darwinian Be a Christian? The Relationship between Science and Religion*. Cambridge: Cambridge University Press.

Russell, Robert John, William R. Stoeger, and George V. Coyne, eds. 1988. *Physics, Philosophy, and Theology: A Common Quest for Understanding*. Vatican City State: Vatican Observatory.

Russell, R. J., N. Murphy and C. J. Isham, eds. 1996. *Quantum Cosmology and the Laws of Nature: Scientific Perspectives on Divine Action*. 2nd ed. Vatican City: Vatican Observatory.

Sanders, E. P. 1993. *The Historical Figure of Jesus*. London: Allen Lane.

Schönborn, Christoph. 2007. *Chance or Purpose: Creation, Evolution and a Rational Faith*. San Francisco: Ignatius Press.

Smolin, Lee. 2006. *The Trouble with Physics: The Rise of String Theory, the Fall of a Science, and What Comes Next*. New York: Mariner.

Swinburne, Richard. 1993. *The Coherence of Theism*. Oxford: Oxford University Press.

———. 2004. *The Existence of God*. 2nd ed. Oxford: Oxford University Press.

van Inwagen, Peter. 2004. *Christian Faith and the Problem of Evil*. Grand Rapids: Eerdmans.

Ward, Keith. 1994. *Religion and Revelation: A Theology of Revelation in the World's Religions*. Oxford: Oxford University Press.

———. 2008. *Why There Almost Certainly Is a God*. Oxford: Lion.

Wilson, E. O. 1978. *On Human Nature*. Cambridge: Harvard University Press.

Woit, Peter. *Not Even Wrong: The Failure of String Theory and the Search for Unity in Physical Law*. New York: Basic Books, 2007.

Wright, N. T. 2003. *The Resurrection of the Son of God*. London: SPCK.

———. 2006. *Simply Christian: Why Christianity Makes Sense*. New York: Harper-Collins.

Index